REJECTED
To
ACCEPTED

*Learning To Love Myself
After Adversity*

> Adore,
> You shared some pretty heavy stuff with me recently and I thought to share this book with you. This book taught me how to love again and just be happy even when there is chaos around me. I hope this does the same for you beautiful.
> Enjoy
> ♥ Destiney ♥

LaSondra Barnes, M.Div.

ISBN 978-1-64492-714-4 (paperback)
ISBN 978-1-64492-715-1 (digital)

Copyright © 2019 by LaSondra Barnes, M.Div.

All rights reserved. No part of this publication may be reproduced, distributed, or transmitted in any form or by any means, including photocopying, recording, or other electronic or mechanical methods without the prior written permission of the publisher. For permission requests, solicit the publisher via the address below.

Christian Faith Publishing, Inc.
832 Park Avenue
Meadville, PA 16335
www.christianfaithpublishing.com

Printed in the United States of America

Dedication

This book is dedicated to my Mom. Thank you for always believing and encouraging me to fulfill my destiny. I would not be the woman that I am without your love, direction, and prayer. I love you beyond words!

Contents

Introduction 7

Chapter 1 Rejection Uncovered 9

Chapter 2 Rejection in Relationships 16

Chapter 3 Breaking Free from Rejection 32

Chapter 4 Transition into Acceptance 43

Chapter 5 Mirror Moments 49

Chapter 6 Accepting Who I Am 65

Chapter 7 Accepting My Past 71

Chapter 8 Transparency 90

Chapter 9 Victory in Action 107

INTRODUCTION

Learning to love myself amid adversity was the toughest yet most fulfilling lessons I accomplished in my life. After experiencing domestic violence and a series of failed and unhealthy relationships, I was left wondering, *Would anyone ever love me?* or *Am I lovable?*

I decided to take a break from dating to focus on loving myself and deepening my relationship with Jesus Christ. In order to fully understand love, I had to go to the source of love, God to receive a clear understanding of His intentions and meaning for it. Through this experience, I found that I had a misunderstanding of love and how it is represented in the world as well as in my life. I asked God to teach me how to love myself and others in the way that He intended.

While on this journey of self-discovery, I was able to allow Jesus to repair the shattered pieces of my heart with the glue of His love. He transformed my thinking by showing me the importance of self-esteem, self-worth, and self-discipline. I learned how to overcome the crippling effects of the rejection that I felt when my dad went from being present to absent in my life by allowing God to step in and fulfill the role of my father. Most importantly, I learned how to genuinely love and celebrate myself while being content in my singleness.

As a youth pastor and life coach, I am always asked questions along the lines of self-love and how to get out of unhealthy relationships and how to grow your relationship with Christ. I have found myself using my own personal struggles and triumphs as examples to help ladies realize their self-worth and deepen their relationship with Christ. I decided to share my story with others because I believe that it will be helpful for people to know that they have the ability to let go of the past, create healthy patterns of future relationships, overcome any circumstance no matter what happened in their lives, and love themselves while in the process of becoming the person God has called them to be.

Chapter 1

Rejection Uncovered

Understanding Rejection

One of the hardest issues for a person to encounter is rejection. Rejection is a problem that has plagued the world and is not specific to a gender, a race, or a socioeconomic group. *Webster's Dictionary* defines *rejection* as "the action of rejecting." The word *reject* is defined as the ability to "refuse to accept, consider, submit to, take for some purpose, or use."

I have found that rejection can be either healthy or harmful. Healthy rejection corresponds to our ability to make choices. We use healthy rejection on a daily basis when we decide between two options—whether it's picking breakfast, what to wear, or how to put on makeup. You have the power to accept or reject anything based on how you want it to affect your life. *Healthy rejection is one that you have control over.* It is necessary in our lives so that we can make decisions that are best for our lives and will allow us to become the person God created us to be.

Unhealthy rejection, on the other hand, causes a person to attach their self-esteem and self-worth to a specific situation which allows them to identify themselves as being lonely, aggressive, unlovable, or depressed. *When unhealthy rejection enters into one's life, it literally robs a person of their identity, replacing it with a blanket of shame that covers the perception of oneself.* This blanket of shame causes one to become afraid of revealing their true identity because they believe that no one will like, want, or love who they are; instead, a false exterior is created.

A person who deals with rejection has a hard time maintaining relationships (platonic or romantic), considering one of the biggest parts of a relationship is transparency. As relationships progress, flaws begin to show. The rejected person gets scared, believing that the other person will not want them after they see their blanket of shame. So instead of revealing it, they create conflicts to cause tension and space, leaving their wounds covered and the other person feeling rejected as well.

An example of unhealthy rejection would be a parent being inconsistent in their child's life. From the time a child is born, there is an immediate longing for the love and acceptance of their parents. As the bonds between child and parent continue to grow, an awareness of self-assurance and trust in that child begins to develop. The relationship that is established between parents and children begins as an infant, molded during adolescence, and tested during teenage years. The time that a child spends with their father during the formative years, whether healthy or unhealthy, will be the pattern that is recreated in future relationships.

If a child does not receive either love, acceptance, or validation, this will causes a void in their heart, leaving them with unmet childhood needs. This void creates the narrative of being unloved by their parent, which causes them to look for love in all the wrong places. As I reflect on my childhood, the relationship with my father was my first encounter with unhealthy rejection, birthed from unmet childhood needs.

My Childhood Experience

From the time I was born up until eight years old, I was a daddy's girl. I absolutely loved my father. To be honest, I felt like I had a better relationship with my father than I did with my mother. I always wanted to be around my father. I thought he was the greatest thing since sliced bread. He made me feel so special, especially when he called me his baby girl. I have an older sister, but to have that distinction made me feel like I mattered to him.

My life changed dramatically when my parents divorced. The day my father moved out was branded as the worst day of my life. I watched my dad silently pack his belongings and slowly walk towards his car. Everyone in my family was home, but no one said anything. We all watched as our family unraveled right before our eyes. I did not want him to leave so, naturally being a daddy's girl, I wanted to go with him.

I waited patiently for him to finish what he was doing so he could pack my stuff. I began to grow impatient after waiting for a long time; I wondered why he did not pack any of my stuff. I was standing on the front porch when he said his final goodbyes and pulled out of our driveway.

He left me, he really left me. Why would he leave me? Wow, I guess I am not good enough for him since he left me with my mom.

While these thoughts were going through my head, it felt like a piece of me died. With this empty space in my heart, rejection decided to take up residence. From that moment, I was always looking for someone or something to replace the void of my father and validate me.

My father went from being a present father—living in our home validating, loving, and directing me—to an absent father who was out of the home. The times we talked, he would promise me something and I would wait and remain hopeful that he would deliver on his word. Sadly, the majority of his promises would go undelivered. Each time I was given an excuse as to why a promise would not be fulfilled, the more my heart broke and the feeling of rejection deepened.

As I transitioned into my teenage years, I found myself longing for love and validation from my father. There were times when he would call or stop by and tell me how proud he was of me and my accomplishments and how I was growing into a beautiful young woman. Those were the best days of my life. I was able to feel like my father wanted me and I was loved.

There were days, which were many, when there was no communication. I struggled, and I felt so unloved. I wanted my old dad back, and I wanted him to be consistent again. Once I got old enough to realize that wasn't going to happen, I learned how to accept my father's part-time love.

As a teen, I learned the art of wearing a mask. I found myself putting my softer side away and allowing my anger and toughness to become my protector. On the inside, I was really hurt; on the outside, I was strong. No one knew that I was searching for validation, acceptance, and love.

I put forth the effort to be the best in school, church, and cheerleading so that I was always receiving validation from someone. *I didn't want to be seen as weak, so I repressed my sadness and disappointment while using perfection as my mask.* With these suppressed emotions, I found myself lashing out in anger toward people. I used my mouth as a weapon to hurt people when I felt attacked or threatened. I wanted people to feel the same way I did on the inside. In those explosive moments, I realized the truth of Proverbs 18:21: "Death and life are in the power of the tongue, and those who love it and indulge it will eat its fruit and bear the consequences of their words."

After a while, I got tired of the mental gymnastics that I was undergoing—one moment nice to people and the next mean and evil. It was time to make a change, so I became more serious about my relationship with Christ. I initially got saved (became a follower of Jesus Christ) at the age of eight. I went to church regularly, but it wasn't enough to just attend church; I needed Jesus to lead my life since I was headed in the wrong direction. I rededicated my life at sixteen years old and received the baptism of the Holy Spirit at Bethlehem Church of God in Christ.

In addition, I received my call to the ministry during that time as well. I knew that Jesus would be with me guiding me every step of the way with this heavy mandate that He has placed on my life. I found peace in the fact that Jesus would always protect, comfort, and love me unconditionally. However, I still longed for my father's love.

It wasn't until my freshman year of college, at Michigan State University, that my relationship with my father began to take a turn for the better. He was ready to be back in my life, and I gladly accepted him. I made sure that I came home every other weekend to spend time with him.

I remember informing my dad that I had an interview for a potential internship with a major accounting firm in Detroit, Michigan, but I did not have a ride there. He told me that he would take me.

I was ecstatic, but I asked him, "Dad, are you sure you can do this? I can just drive your car there if it is too much."

"Sondra, I would be honored to take you to your interview."

During this time, he was battling systemic scleroderma, so he was limited in the things that he could do. For him to be willing to do this for me was major. He was in constant pain daily and had limited mobility. Once he told me that his skin felt like it was on fire and he had no way of cooling down the sensation.

The day of my interview came, and my dad picked me up from my dorm, Hubbard Hall, to head to Detroit. In that moment, I felt so special because my dad was making me a priority even though he was in pain. After the interview was over, we spent the remainder of the day together. This is a memory that I will never forget.

Over the next year, my dad's health began to decline. I would continue to go see him every other weekend and make sure I called him on a regular basis. Fast forward a year and a half later, my mom informed me that my dad was back in the hospital and I needed to see him. For months, I had been praying for God to miraculously heal my father but it seemed like that was not happening.

I remember going to see my father in the hospital, and he was really sick and frail. I talked to my dad for about thirty minutes, and then he started giving me advice and encouragement. He told me how proud he was of me, how he wanted me to not stop until I reached my goals, and that he loved me. I felt like this was coming from a different place than normal.

He then said, "Sondra, this is my last surgery. I am not coming in here anymore."

I replied, "I believe that, Dad. I've been praying for God for a miraculous healing for you."

He then said something that I was not expecting. "That's nice, but God will not override your prayers for mine. I don't think a miraculous healing would do me any good. This is the thorn in my flesh. If I was healed right now, I don't know if I would be living for God the way I am now."

I was shocked by his comments. I didn't want to believe what he was saying, so I quickly changed the subject to my finals. I told my dad that finals started on Monday and I had been studying for them, so I was ready. He gave me some additional encouragement and said that he needed some rest.

We hugged and we exchanged I love yous. As I headed toward the door, my dad said, "Bye, Sondra."

I stopped, "No, see you later."

This was a thing that we started doing. I remember him saying bye before, and I didn't want to hear that from him anymore. I left the hospital and went back to school to prep for my finals.

A few days later, I kept getting cryptic calls from my older brother and sister asking me about my visit with Dad. They wanted to know how he was, what we talked about, and what his condition was when I left. I was so focused on studying that I answered their questions without giving their questions a second thought.

The next morning, I was packing my bag to head to my math final, and there was a knock at my door. I went to answer it, and I saw my brother and my mom.

My heart sunk, "What are you doing here? I am getting ready to leave for my math final."

My brother walks through the door first and looks at me and says with a shaky voice, "It's about Dad."

Tears begin to run down his face, and in that moment, I knew why they were there. My dad has died. I let out a scream from the bottom of my stomach, fell on the floor, and cried. Not my dad! Not now, not while we are finally having a good relationship. My dad has left me again.

After my dad's passing, I felt a variety of feelings, ranging from sadness to anger. All the progress we had made was undone. I was lost and alone. The feeling of rejection that I met when my parents divorced, quickly reemerged and I didn't understand why every man I loved left me. It must be that I am genuinely not loved.

Love to me was consistency. I felt like I didn't get that from my dad, as he was always in and out of my life. I think rejection painted a negative picture of my dad's love in my head. I only focused on the things he didn't do or how he wasn't there for me. I harbored those lies as truth: it allowed for my perspective of myself, love, and my father to be tainted. The emptiness of rejection took over my life, leaving me aching for love and acceptance. I was back to looking for love in all of the wrong places again.

If you can relate to my experience, I want to take a moment and encourage you. No matter what heartache you have experienced from childhood or adulthood, I want you to know that YOU ARE LOVED, YOU ARE NOT A MISTAKE, AND YOU ARE ENOUGH.

I recognize the importance of a father to a young lady. He is to instill in her identity, self-esteem, and self-worth. To not receive that information will leave a woman searching for love in all the wrong places. No matter what kind of relationship you have with your natural father, you have a Heavenly Father who loves you. Psalm 27:10 says, "Although my father and my mother have abandoned me, Yet the Lord will take me up [adopt me as His child]" (AMP).

If your natural father never tells you he loves, you know that you have a Heavenly Father that loves and wants you to embrace and accept His love.

CHAPTER 2

Rejection in Relationships

My Breaking Point—Domestic Abuse

Fall 2006, two years after my father's death, I put my relationship with God on the back burner and started fulfilling the lusts of my flesh. I found out the true meaning of 2 Peter 5:8, which states, "Be sober, be vigilant; because your adversary the devil walks about like a roaring lion, seeking whom he may devour." All the voids from my past came back in full force, and I found love, or what I thought was love, in all the wrong people.

I dated emotionally unavailable men expecting them to replace my father's love. I compromised my morals, values, and Christian standards, all for the sake of getting them to love me. I confused love with lust. I thought that if I gave those men my body, they would give me love. When these relationships would end, I would automatically go back to the unloved and rejected little girl wanting her father's attention.

While the pain grew, I remember hearing the enemy say, "LaSondra, you are unlovable. Every man you have ever loved left you." Once I allowed this statement to rest in my mind, I no longer knew how to fight because my past experiences proved that this statement was the truth. My self-worth was so distorted that I believed God did not love me.

I found myself in a position I had assumed far too often in my last relationship in college—on the floor pinned down by my boyfriend. I was being abused by him because I did not follow his instructions and do what he said. Those moments were torture because he would bite me as hard as he could from head to toe and then laugh about it.

The first few times I tried to fight back but my 5'2" and 140-pound body was no match against his 6'2" and 170-pound build. After being physically, verbally, and psychologically abused on a regular basis, I figured that it was easier for me to just do what he said. Honestly, I was scared of him and he knew it.

At the beginning of our relationship, I thought his aggressive "bad boy" attitude was cute and alluring. I never imagined he would focus his aggression and disrespect toward me. What sane person would do these things to another human being, especially the one they supposedly loved.

The abuse did not start out intense, it was subtle with negative comments here and there, a shove, or heavy wrestling. The moment we slept together and he moved in, everything changed. He told me that I was his property and it was imperative that I comply with his commands or I would pay. I thought he was joking, so I laughed it off.

Later on, we were walking back to my apartment, and I happened to walk a few steps in front of him, and he yanked my arm so hard I thought it was going to come out of the socket.

I yelled, "What are you doing? That hurts!"

He replied, "Don't you ever disrespect me again by walking in front of me."

Once we got inside of my apartment, I paid for that mistake.

While enduring his abusive episodes, a part of me wanted to leave because I knew that I did not deserve this type of treatment, but we loved each other and every relationship has its tough spots. Every day we stayed together, my self-esteem, self-worth, and identity slowly decreased. He made sure to tell me what he did not like about me, what I needed to change, and how no one would ever love or want me because I was damaged goods.

Even after hearing such horrible words, I was still determined to make the relationship work. He shared with me that he had experienced a very rough childhood, so I wanted to be the one person to show him what true love looked like. I thought this was the price I would have to pay in order to help him become a better man. If I can be honest, I was tired of having a trail of failed relationships, so I sacrificed my well-being to prove to myself that I could have a successful one.

For the next few months, I tried my best to hide my bruises from everyone with whom I was in contact with. I was so ashamed that I did not want anyone to know that I—Ms. Independent, saved and sanctified, educated, "take no mess" Sondra—was being tossed around like a ragdoll and had no strength to stand up for myself. Since it was fall, I would wear my black fleece jacket zipped all the way to the top to cover the bruises on my neck, chest, and arms. I frequently cancelled doctors' appointments and missed classes because of the pain I was in.

I could not allow my peers or doctors to see me in extreme amounts of pain; they would have known I was being abused. I was so stressed out that I lost my appetite, and I started losing weight. I went from a size 8 to a size 3 in two months. (I have never been that small in my life.) I started distancing myself from everybody and did not let my friends come over to my apartment.

A few of my friends noticed that I changed in size, personality, and behavior. They would ask me, "Sondra, is everything all right?" or "You don't seem as happy as you use to be?" or "Missed seeing you in class today, are you okay?" I would make up some excuse to answer their questions. I was consumed with so much guilt and shame that I felt like if I told them what was really going on, they would judge me and make me feel worse than what I was already feeling.

After a month of trying to continue this balancing act and keeping my lies straight, I realized that I could not deal with this torment any longer and I needed help. I had to tell my friends what was going on and get that off of my chest. I invited one of my good friends over to my apartment and told her the truth about my relationship with my boyfriend.

I was ready for the ridicule and disappointment that I had feared. Surprisingly, I didn't receive any of that. She did not judge me; she was truly concerned. She looked me in the eyes and asked, "Why are you staying with him since he is doing these things to you?"

I replayed this question over and over in my head. I told her the truth, "I am too scared to leave. He told me that if I were to leave him, he would kill me."

She began to cry and said that she would be praying for me to get the strength to leave and for God to protect me.

When my best friend found out, it was a different story. She knew something was going on in our relationship; she didn't like him from the beginning. One day, she randomly showed up to my apartment, and my boyfriend and I were right in the midst of a fight. She began banging on the door when she heard what was going on.

That moment the fight was over, he grabbed his stuff, opened the door, looked at my best friend, and stormed past her. My best friend walked into the opened door, looked around, and said to me, "I'm only going to tell you this once. YOU ARE BETTER THAN THIS! I'm not going to beg you to leave him. I know that when you are ready to leave, you will. Just know that YOU ARE MORE WORTH THAN THIS." After that, she left.

She left me sitting in my apartment replaying her words in my mind. *"You are worth more than this."*

"Am I really worth more than this?" I said out loud to myself as I walked into the bathroom. I looked in the mirror, and for the first time, I saw myself. I was frail because I wasn't eating, there was sadness in my eyes, bruises all over my body, and an overall feeling of hopelessness. Wow, I could not believe that the reflection in the mirror was me.

In that moment, I realized that through the course of this relationship, I became a broken and battered woman. This is not what I signed up for. I did not know that *this* would be the price to pay to prove a point to myself.

As I stood in the shower, the hot water began to soothe my bruised skin, tears began to run down my face, and I wept. I was saddened by my own reflection, and I began to ask God for help. I started singing a line out of Fred Hammond's song, "Please Don't Pass Me By": "Jesus, I need you, please don't pass me by. I know that I'm broken but you can heal me, Jesus, Jesus, I'm calling you. Might be worth much, but I'm still willing, Jesus, Jesus, I'm calling you."

I knew that if I did not call on Jesus to get me out of this situation, I was not going to make it. I could not believe that I let myself get into this situation. I was embarrassed, but I did not know how to get out. I asked God to give me the strength to get out of that relationship. I knew it was not going to be easy, but I knew it was necessary for me to do.

When my boyfriend arrived back to my apartment, he brought me flowers as a peace offering and apologized for his actions. He was so remorseful for his actions, he promised that he would not lose his temper like that again. He began crying and begging me not to leave him. He said that while he was away, he prayed and asked God for help. He realized that he made a huge mistake and didn't want to lose me.

He told me that I was the best thing that has ever happened to him. That I made him a better man. He asked me to give him some time to show me that he has changed.

Wow, these are the things I had been waiting to hear from him. He has to be telling the truth because he has never done anything like this before. Maybe he is really going to change. Maybe this relationship can really work out, I thought to myself.

I decided to give him another chance, since everyone makes mistakes. He deserves grace. Right?

A few weeks later, I realized that taking him back was the wrong decision. He quickly fell back into his patterns of verbal, psychological, and physical abuse. This time, the rage level increased to dramatic levels.

We were having another argument and he was standing in front of me and said, "I am so sick and tired of you. I am going to have someone murder you. Yep, that's what I'm going to do. This will be the last time you see me." He proceeded to grab his things and left the apartment.

I was left standing in the middle of the floor, shaking from head to toe. *Could he really kill me?*

I was reminded of the time that he tried to a few weeks ago, but he didn't. Was he serious? Who was he going to get to do this? I remembered that he introduced me to a person whom he knew from his old neighborhood who was a hit man for a gang. I always thought he was lying about that but not anymore.

My boyfriend was a man of his word, so I knew he was going to send someone to kill me. I felt it in my bones. That was the first time I felt death coming toward me, and I did not know what to do. So I started crying, praying, and reading my Bible on the floor of my dining room. I read every scripture that I could find concerning life, protection, salvation, peace, justice, love—anything I could find. I needed a miracle, and I needed it fast.

I prayed for hours, and once I was done, I called my mom and all my close friends and told them that I loved them. I did not go into detail about the reason for the call; I just wanted them to know that I loved them. As much as I wanted to live, I had a feeling that I would not be alive the next day. The next day comes and sure enough there was a knock on the door. I debated answering it, but I did.

In that moment, I stood face to face with my boyfriend's hit man friend. My heart skipped a beat in my chest. I said a silent prayer, "Jesus, please help me."

I turned on the widest smile I could conjure up and said, "Hey, friend, how are you?"

He responded, barely looking at me, "Yo, where is my boy at?"

I said, "He's not here. I have not seen him since yesterday."

"Can I come in?" he said.

Looking around, I replied, "Sure."

As he entered into my apartment, he asked me, "What have you been up to?"

Trying to remain calm, I said, "Just school, work, preaching, and loving Jesus."

He looked surprised and said, "Preaching? You are a preacher?"

I said, "Yes, I've been preaching since I was sixteen years old. I love to preach. You know I love me some Jesus. I'm also a chaplain in the gospel choir."

Looking amazed, he said, "Wow, I didn't know you were a preacher. I guess that's why you are so nice. So you are in school and you're a preacher. You are a really good woman."

I said, "Why, thank you! I'm trying my best to be the woman that God has called me to be."

Then he said, "You are a good woman. Tell my boy that I couldn't do it." He turned around and walked out of my apartment and disappeared down the stairwell.

I immediately started crying as I shut the door and said, "THANK YOU, JESUS, FOR SAVING MY LIFE!" I worshipped and cried for about an hour. I was so grateful that God actually delivered me from the hands of death.

About an hour later, my boyfriend arrived to my apartment. Slowly opening the door, he was shocked when he saw me. He asked, "What are you doing here?"

I replied, "I live here, remember?"

He said, "Did anybody come over here for me?"

I responded, "Yes, your friend came by a few hours ago and told me to tell you that he couldn't do it."

My boyfriend rolled his eyes at me and walked out the door, cussing under his breath.

While he was away, I finally realized that I needed to get out of this relationship for good. That was not healthy for me. I allowed every aspect of my life to be taken advantage of because I believed that he loved me. I was convinced that I did not deserve anything better.

Ready to Go!

That next day, I went to church, ready for Jesus to make me whole again. I remember going to the altar for prayer, weeping from my brokenness. From that moment, transformation started to occur in my life. I heard the Holy Spirit speak to my heart these words: "Daughter, I love you, I accept you, and you are not forgotten."

I could feel the power of God moving all over my body, and I knew that I was alive again and I did not want to be devoured by the devil anymore. I asked Jesus to fill every void in my life and make me into the woman whom He created me to become. I desired the clarity of His voice, the boldness of His Spirit, and the closeness of His love. I knew this journey to freedom was going to be tough, but I was ready to go on the ride. I left church with a new determination to live and get out of that abusive situation. I was aware that Jesus would always protect, comfort, and love me unconditionally.

As the following week started, I was silently gaining my strength and confidence back. My boyfriend must have sensed that I was changing. By the middle of the week, he was back into one of his destructive moods.

He started an argument with me over nothing and said to me, "You can't live without me."

I quickly shot back the lyrics to a song by Vicki Winans, "Yes, I can. As long as I got King Jesus, I don't need anybody else."

I could not finish my sentence before he came over and body-slammed me to the floor, pinning me down, "Where is your God at now?"

I was completely frozen and shocked. Why would he make a statement like that? "Where is your God at now?" I thought he was a godly man. I vividly remember meeting him at my church one Sunday after service.

In that split second, I realized that this guy never really loved Jesus; he was using that as a cover to deceive Christian women. I wanted more than anything for God to give me the strength of Samson and show him exactly where my God was. Unfortunately, that did not happen.

I screamed, "Get off me."

He laughed and said, "No. Matter a fact, I'm going to get you pregnant. You will be stuck with me forever."

I told him to get off me, but he ignored me. I started rocking back and forth, trying to get myself free, but I could not. In my mind, I am thinking, *Where are you, Jesus? Please, don't let this happen to me.*

Again, I screamed, "Get off me, please!"

He said, "Shut up and move your leg over."

As I continued to try to squirm around, I pleaded with him one last time, "Please, don't do this."

"Shut up and enjoy me getting you pregnant."

Unable to move, I lay on the ground in disbelief that he was sexually assaulting me.

Once he finished, he said, "You better not kill my baby either." Then he got up and walked away from me.

I felt completely numb and worthless. I went into the bathroom, locked the door, turned on the water and cried. I had endured a lot of painful moments in the last few months. How dare he take the very thing that I did not have a problem freely giving to him?

In my disappointment, I blamed myself for allowing this happen. If I am pregnant, I do not want to be stuck with this man for the rest of my life.

I silently prayed, "Lord, I need a miracle. I can't be attached to this man anymore."

During those moments, all the fear I had for him turned into contempt and hate. I felt dirty, but I was more determined than ever to get out of our relationship. I finally reached my limit and had enough. I was ready to leave him. As I showered, I prayed for God to give me a surefire plan get out of my relationship and not return.

A week later, God began to work things out on my behalf. Unbeknownst to me, my sister had called my mom and told her that something was wrong with me and she needed to come to Michigan State and check on me. They didn't know exactly what was wrong with me, but they knew that I was in trouble.

My mom decided to come up and visit me. When she saw me, she asked me about my boyfriend, and I stuttered and told her, "Mom, I hate him." I guess her motherly instincts kicked in, and she stayed with me for the next week, driving forty-five minutes back and forth to work.

During that time, my mom didn't press me for information. She just loved on me and prayed for me. My mom is a prayer warrior, and I knew that if she was there, then I would be just fine. I would wake up to her, praying and pleading the blood of Jesus over me.

Growing up, she would lay hands on me and my sibling while we were sleeping, anoint our heads with oil, and pray a powerful prayer over us. It felt good to know that my mom was still covering me with her love, prayers, and strength. I am so grateful for having a mother who is a Christian woman. She taught me the importance of knowing God for myself and how to utilize the spiritual disciplines of prayer, worship, scripture memorization, journaling, and Bible Study. Being able to watch God move in my mom's life gave me the encouragement to know that Jesus can do the same for me.

There is nothing like a mother's love. Just by her staying with me let me know that I was not alone and that my well-being matters to her. My mom told me that real love doesn't hurt and that if you are afraid of being in your own home, then something is wrong. I didn't see my boyfriend at all while she was there, and I felt empowered.

After she left, I knew that I was ready to end the relationship. I did not care what he was going to say or do; I did not want to be a part of that dysfunction any longer. It was imperative that I loved myself more than I loved him or this relationship. It was time for him to go; he was not paying any bills anyway.

He must have been watching my apartment; he came back as soon as my mom left. He was ready to pick up our dysfunctional relationship right where we left off, and I was not having it. By the middle of the next week, I told him that he needed to get his things and leave.

Immediately, he tried his standard fear tactics on me, and that didn't work. He said, "You're not scared of me anymore, are you?"

I said, "No, so get your stuff and get out. If you decide to put your hands on me, someone is going to die today, and it's not going to be me. So what do you want to do?"

Shocked that I was standing up for myself, he postured himself over me and just stood there. That moment, honestly, I was ready to fight to the point of death.

I told him, "Go ahead and put your hands on me. I have had enough. I promise you, someone is going to die today, and IT WILL NOT BE ME. TRY ME!"

He decided to walk away from me and said, "Stop playing and go cook me some dinner."

I replied, "Okay. Just FYI, I will be poisoning you from this day forward. So you will die one way or the other. Trust me! So what would you like to eat?"

He could not believe what I just said. He started crying and said, "Babe, I can't leave. I don't have anywhere to go."

I responded, "That is not my problem or my concern. You need to leave, so get your stuff and get out—*now!*"

He must have seen the look in my eye and said, "I didn't know you were this crazy. I'm out!" and then he packed his bags and left.

I was so surprised that it only took me standing up for myself for him to leave. I was expecting some explosive fight or something. I guess he was nothing more than a bully. After composing myself, I called my best friend and told her what happened between me and my boyfriend. She was ready to fight! I calmed her down and told her it was not worth it. She thought it would be best if I stayed with her for a few days, just in case he tried to come back and do something crazy. I agreed with her, packed up my bags, and stayed at her apartment for a few days.

It felt so good to be out of that situation.

Telling the Truth

I might have been physically out of the relationship, but I was not mentally out of it. I knew that I had a lot of work to do to rebuild myself emotionally, physically, and mentally. In order to properly heal, I knew the first thing I had to do was to tell the people, closest to me, the truth.

I had to tell my family what happened to me. There was no way I could act like nothing happened; my mom and sister were not going to rest until they found out. On top of that, Tiya (my best friend) had given me a deadline to tell my family. She said, if I didn't tell, she would.

I was on the clock, so I had to come clean. I decided that the following week, I was going to go home and tell my family. With the amount of guilt, shame, and disappointment I was feeling, I thought that I could keep this secret and no one else would find out about it. I guess Jesus had another plan.

I was at church barely listening to the sermon. My mind would not stop replying some of the horrible events that took place weeks prior. I was fighting with the inward torture and hoped that Jesus would intervene as soon as possible.

I was brought back to reality when I heard the associate pastor begin his altar call and say, "The Lord is saying there is someone in here who has been sexually assaulted, and they are struggling with guilt and shame. Jesus is here to restore all that was taken from you. It was not your fault."

My heart nearly jumped out of my chest when I heard that. *Who told him I was sexually assaulted?* I was thinking. *Wait, he couldn't be talking about me! It has to be someone else.*

He proceeded to say, "I am not moving until you come up here. We are not going to judge you. We will wait for you."

My heart was racing. I started praying, "Lord, I know you don't want me to go up there. I can't. If I do, everyone will know what has been going on, and I will be sat down. I am a part of the leadership team here at the church—I am going to lose everything. Please, God, don't make me go up there. I'm sorry. I don't want be embarrassed. They are going to look at me differently."

I could hear the Holy Spirit speak to my heart, "*Go up there.*"

I started bargaining with the Lord, "Jesus, I promise I will tell my mom today, I will. I won't keep it a secret anymore." I was determined not to go up there, hoping someone else would out themselves, and I keep my assault a secret.

I kept feeling Jesus tug at my heartstrings; I knew I could not be disobedient, and I had to go to the altar. I said, "Okay, Lord, if he makes the call one more time, I will go up there. You have been there for me, so the least I can do is be obedient."

Sure enough, the associate pastor made the call one more time.

I walked down to the altar, shaking and weeping. The walk to the front of the church felt like it was a mile away. I felt the lyrics to Cece Winan's song "Alabaster Box" come alive in that moment.

> The room grew still as she made her way to Jesus. She stumbled through the tears that make her blind. She felt such pain. Some spoke in anger, heard folks whisper, there's no place here for her kind. Still on she came through the shame that flushed her face, until at last she knelt before his feet. And though she spoke no words, everything she said was heard, as she poured her love for the master from her box of Alabaster. And I've come to pour my praise on Him like oil from Mary's Alabaster Box. Don't be angry if I wash His feet with my tears and I dry them with my hair. You weren't there the night He found me, you did not feel what I felt, when He wrapped His loving arms around me. And you don't know the cost of the oil in my Alabaster box.

Once I arrived to the front of the church, I knelt down and let out a cry from the depth of my heart. I knew that I couldn't carry that weight around anymore. No matter what the negative thoughts continuously said, in my mind, I knew that Jesus loved me and had a plan for my life. Going to the altar was the first step of removing the shame that was controlling my life.

As my mind reflected on the past, the associate pastor came up to me and prayed a powerful prayer over me. Once church was over, he came up to me and asked if I could meet him in his office. I replied yes. I knew what was next; I had to tell him what happened.

I had a pretty good relationship with the pastors of my church, so this information was new to them. As we set in his office, I told him that I was sexually assaulted and in an abusive relationship with my ex-boyfriend for the past few months.

He was shocked. He called in the senior pastor to inform him of the conversation. They asked me a ton of questions. They told me that they were going to speak to my ex about this matter. They would like to set up a follow-up meeting later in the week to further discuss the next steps. I was fine with that. I knew that I had truth on my side, so I was not worried. I left church, empowered and ready to tell my family about my situation.

The following week, I called my mom. As the seconds ticked away while the phone was ringing, I was telling myself, "Sondra, you can do this. You have to tell her the truth. No more secrets." Keeping secrets is what caused me to be in this place, so it was time to remove the cover and walk in freedom by telling the truth.

My mom answered the phone like normal, with love and patience. And asked, "How are you doing?"

I let out a huge sigh and said, "Not good."

"What's going on?" she replied with great concern.

I replied, "Well, I'm being sat down at church."

"Why are you being sat down at church?" she said.

"Well, the pastors found out about me and my ex."

"What did they find out?" This time, her reply was filled with more concern.

I took a deep breath and said, "For the last few months, my ex has been abusing me. He moved into my place and wouldn't leave. It wasn't until you came up and stayed with me that he left. After that, I was able to get enough strength to walk away from the situation." Tears were flowing down my face, and I was full of shame.

I was overcome with shame because I knew better. I knew that my mom raised me better than that. I knew that that information would be a letdown to her, a woman whom I have admired all my life.

However, her voice was wrapped in love and action when "Oh no, Sondra. I knew something was going on, but I didn't think this was it. Are you okay? Do you feel safe? Why didn't you tell me? I am so sorry that you had to go through this alone." She was in tears now.

"Mom, I wanted to tell you, but I was so scared. I didn't want to get you guys involved and something happened to you. He told me that he was going to kill me. Well, he actually tried a few times. I didn't have the "strength to fight back."

"When I tried to stand up for myself, he would intimidate me so that I would cower down in fear. I wanted him to leave, but he wouldn't. Mom, I don't feel safe up here by myself. I know that I have to keep it moving, but I don't want to be here anymore."

"Sondra, come home. You don't have to stay in East Lansing. You can come home."

"Thanks, Mom."

As I ended the conversation, I sat there, and I knew that my mom loved me and wanted nothing but the best for me.

As I put the situation behind me, the pastors called, asking for another meeting. I arrived to the pastors' office and we had small talk but then started discussing the abusive relationship. They informed me that they spoke to my ex-boyfriend, and he denied all allegations of physical and sexual abuse.

Of course he would, I thought to myself.

Then the pastor said, "Are you *sure* this happened to you?"

I looked at him with disappointment and anger written all over my face. "Yes, I'm sure. Why would I lie about this? Why would I lie and say that the worst thing that would ever happen to a woman happened to me? Why would I lie when I know that I will be sat down because of it? Why would I lie?

"Haven't you noticed that I have changed over these last few months? Have you ever wondered why I always wore that black fleece jacket zipped all the way to the top all the time? Have you noticed how I always look down and don't smile anymore? Have you noticed that I get extremely uncomfortable being in close proximity to men? Have you noticed that I have lost a dramatic amount of weight in a short period of time?"

By that time, I was crying.

"Pastor, I have been abused by this guy for months. He has taken advantage of me in every way imaginable. This man tried to kill me! I am not lying about this. If you still don't believe me, then ask Lindsey or my best friend Tiya or my mom. They will tell you what has been going on with me."

I grabbed my things, ready to storm out of his office.

He said, "I'm sorry, daughter. I didn't know you went through all of this. We will do whatever it takes to make you feel safe."

Grabbing a tissue, I said, "Thank you."

He told me that I would be sat down because I did not have any integrity.

I replied, "I was expecting you to say that."

Honestly, that is understandable. You can't stand up and preach about something that you are not living. So I get it. Preaching in front of the church was the least of my worries at that moment. I planned on using that time to truly heal mind, body, and soul. By the end of the week, I was informed that the pastors asked my ex-boyfriend to leave the church. That was a great feeling.

If you have ever found yourself in a relationship where your partner gets angry so easily that you feel like you are walking on eggshells; if he calls you belittling or disrespectful names; teases you in a hurtful way while playing it off as a joke; maybe you have lost friends or no longer see some family members because of your partner; or he hits, shoves, or uses force to restrain you; then it is an unhealthy, abusive relationship.

This kind of relationship is not God ordained and is slowly killing you from the inside out. You do not deserve to be treated in this manner. You are a child of the Most High God, and you should be treated with respect and honor.

Chapter 3

Breaking Free from Rejection

My Healing Journey Begins

This relationship left me emotionally at the lowest place in my life. To me, I felt like life was moving in slow motion, and I spent a lot of time questioning myself, trying to figure out why I keep attracting the same type of person (with a different name) yet receiving the same outcome. Within those relationships, I found myself giving all that I had with the expectation of someone loving me. That's all I wanted. I just wanted someone to love, validate, and protect me. Isn't that the expectation women are supposed to have for a man?

A man is supposed to be the knight in shining armor, fixing all of my problems while simultaneously filling the voids of my heart. This was the expectation that I placed on every guy I dated. I wanted them to do things for me that they were not created to do. I wanted someone to love me so that I could feel lovable. For most of my life, I secretly felt like I was not loveable or enough to be loved. I thought that if I gave people what I secretly desired, they would give it back to me. At the point of breaking, I decided that it was time to take a break from dating because what I have been doing was *not* working!

Encounter with God

Once my semester was over, my mom decided that I needed to get away from Michigan to clear my head while visiting my sister in Portland, Oregon, for the winter break. While on the plane, I was lost in my thoughts; ultimately, I knew that I wanted to heal, move on, and not get into anymore unhealthy relationships or feel rejection. I just didn't know where to begin.

This goal was bigger than anything I could accomplish on my own, so I decided to leave it there. "I can't deal with this right now," I told myself as I turned on my Zune (Microsoft's version of an iPod), closed my eyes, and relaxed. A song by Deitrick Haddon entitled "I'm The One" came on, and these lyrics stopped me directly in my tracks:

> I've been watchin' you and holdin' you all of your life, even through wrong and right, but I'll still love you, hate to see you hurt goin' through so much pain, it don't have to be this way, just let me love you. I can be the calm to your storm, I can be the wave when you're lost, I can be the smile when you're down, just reach out for me I'm here, I can give you joy so sweet, it will make your love for me so deep, just look up and close your eyes, and reach out for me. I'm the one that you're searching for, but the question is, do you want to be loved? I can ease the pain, I can stop the rain, but the question is, do you want to be loved?
>
> Here's my resume, take a look I'm qualified, it was me who gave you life, that's how much I love you, you can search all over but you will never find, I'm the way the truth the light, Why don't you choose me?, why don't you just call on me, I'll come runnin' (I'll come runnin'), I'll meet you at the, I'll meet you at the point of

your need, And I will answer (I will answer), Yes I will, Just realize that I'm the one. I'm the one that you're searching for, but the question is, do you want to be loved? I can ease the pain, I can stop the rain, but the question is, do you want to be loved?

As the song ended, I knew for sure God was speaking directly to me through this song. He asked me a question that I longed for a man to ask me, "Do you want to be loved?" Yes, I want to be loved! But I knew that there was more to this question than a superficial answer. I thought to myself, what would happen if I allowed God to truly love me the way that He is describing in the song? What would he do when I revealed my broken pieces? Would he just leave me like every other man in my life?

I wrestled because secretly I believed that God only loved me sympathetically, that He had to love me but it's not by choice—it's because He created me. I remember hearing people say, "If no one loves you, know that God loves you." To me, that sounds like he is the last resort. However, I wasn't sensing that in that moment; it was something completely different.

I prayed to God, "Lord, I am answering your question. *Yes*, I want to be loved by you completely. My eyes are focused on you, teach me what love is, how to love myself and others the way you intended. I am desperate for you and your love. Please wrap your arms around me and lead me through this process. Lord, I need your strength to endure this journey of healing. I trust you with all of my heart and I thank you for remaining faithful to me even though I am not always faithful to you."

I opened my Bible to Isaiah 41:10

> Do not fear [anything], for I am with you; Do not be afraid, for I am your God. I will strengthen you, be assured I will help you; I will certainly take hold of you with My righteous right hand [a hand of justice, of power, of victory, of salvation]. (AMP)

Then the Lord spoke to my heart and said, "This journey is not going to be easy, but I am going to walk you through this process of healing. When you are finished, you will understand my love for you."

A sense of peace swept over me, and I was comforted. I came to the realization that I don't have to work for His love; He is freely giving it to me. It doesn't matter what I have endured or how I felt about myself; He was willing—wanted me, even—when I was at my lowest point. *He wanted to love me*!

I then turned to Matthew 11:28–29, which says, "Come unto me, all you who labor and are heavy laden, and I will give you rest. Take my yoke upon you and learn from me, for I am gentle and lowly in heart, and you will find rest for your souls." I have read this verse for many years, but that day, it was different. It was like an invitation to do a strength exchange from God. I was ready for rest. I really needed it.

My Perspective on Love

I remember being in the car, and the Holy Spirit spoke to my heart, "*How do you define love?*"

How do I define love? That's a good question. Once I arrived at my sister's house, I grabbed my prayer journal and started answering the question. *How do I define love?*

I defined love as an emotional feeling or an affection one has for a person, place, or thing. Love can be displayed in multiple ways—romantic, familial, or the way you care for items. I think that love is an emotion that we are introduced to from the time we were born and is nurtured all throughout our lives. Love to me is consistency. I feel loved when a person is consistent in my life.

The next question came to me, "*How do you feel about love?*"

How do I feel about love? Lord, why are you asking me this? I could feel my heart beating fast because I knew that the God was asking me these questions so He could begin surgery on my thinking.

I wrote down, "Honestly, Lord, there was a point in time when I held the *idea* of love in high regard, but after experiencing rejection from my father and failed relationships with the men in my life, I think love has failed me. I don't think I am lovable. If I was, I would be in a healthy loving relationship or have a strong relationship with my father."

After I finished writing that statement, I took a minute to reflect on what I just wrote. "Whoa, where did this come from?" I said to myself.

I never knew that I felt like love had failed me. I started to cry because I was completely vulnerable in that moment. I sat there silently and waited for God to respond, and the negative thoughts started playing in my mind, and I heard, *"See, I keep telling you that no one loves you. God doesn't even love you. If he did, he would have said something by now."*

I started to get nervous because I didn't want to believe these thoughts, not this time. I started playing a worship song I waited for God to respond.

God's Perspective on Love

John 3:16 came to mind, "For God so loved the world that whosoever believes in Him will not perish but have everlasting life."

God responds, *"Love has never failed you. Love has been in existence before creation. It was love that created the world, it was love that created man from the dust of the ground, it was love's voice that walked in the Garden with Adam in the cool of the day. Love can never fail you because I am love."*

In order to get a better understanding of God's perspective on love, I looked up the definition in the Greek language because that's the original language the New Testament was written in. The Greek word for love in John 3:16 is *agape*. This is the spiritual sense of love and is defined as an unconditional affection that desires only the good for a person. It has a consuming passion for the well-being of others. This type of love delights in giving and keeps consistent affection, regardless of what the other person is doing. This is the only type of love that will allow us to truly love ourselves from the inside out because it is not based on our emotions (which changes) but on God (which is unchanging).

I went on to find other scriptures that use *agape* as *love* and I found First Corinthians 13:4–8:

> *Love* endures long and is patient and kind; *love* never is envious nor boils over with jealousy, is not boastful or vainglorious, does not display itself haughtily. It is not conceited (arrogant and inflated with pride); it is not rude (unmannerly) and does not act unbecomingly. *Love* (God's love in us) does not insist on its own rights or its own way, for it is not self-seeking; it is not touchy or fretful or resentful; it takes no account of the evil done to it [it pays no attention to a suffered wrong]. It does not rejoice at injustice and unrighteousness, but rejoices when right and truth prevail. *Love* bears up under anything and everything that comes, is ever ready to believe the best of every person, its hopes are fadeless under all circumstances, and it endures everything [without weakening]. *Love* never fails [never fades out or becomes obsolete or comes to an end]. As for prophecy (the gift of interpreting the divine will and purpose), it will be fulfilled and pass away; as for tongues, they will be destroyed and cease; as for knowledge, it will pass away [it will lose its value and be superseded by truth]. (AMP; italics added)

Based on this scripture, I could no longer hold to the idea that love had failed me. The hardships I have experienced was not a true representation of love, especially God's love. It was time to embrace God's love and change my definition and perspective of love, how I saw and valued myself.

Embracing God's Love

Embracing God's love challenged me to change my mind-set by allowing Jesus to offer me a new view of life. I had to decide if I was really ready to let go of how I viewed and defined love, my perception of self, and my self-worth. Even though it was formed by rejection, that misinformation was what I deemed as truth.

I'm going to be honest, changing my mind-set was hard. What God was asking me to do was forsake the story that I have known for my whole life, the one that I learned to cope with or at least tried to cope. I had to forsake the things that have held me captive for so long.

I found myself praying Psalm 51:10 and Romans 12:2 all the time. I would say, "Create in me a clean heart. O God, and renew a right and steadfast spirit within me. Lord, help me not be conformed to this world [any longer with its superficial values and customs], but be transformed and progressively changed [as I mature spiritually] by the renewing of my mind [focusing on godly values and ethical attitudes], so that my may prove [for myself] what the will of God is, that which is good and acceptable and perfect [in His plan and purpose for me]."

My Choices

Embracing God's love is my foundation. As I embraced His love, I was able to see the difference between what is good and evil. Those are the things that bring life and death into my life. It's not about being legalistic; it's about freedom. It's about living every day full of life but with awareness. It's like losing weight—everyday temptation is there, and you have to make the choice to work out and eat right.

I am capable of making right choices. I had to stop blaming everyone else for my current situation. Yes, people played a role however, I had the ability to make choices. In order for anything to happen, I had to make the choice to say yes or no.

Forgiveness

When you decide to forgive, you are making a conscious choice to change your attitude about wanting revenge or resentment. Matthew 6:14–15 says,

> For if you forgive others their trespasses [their reckless and willful sins], your heavenly Father will also forgive you. But if you do not forgive others [nurturing your hurt and anger with the result that it interferes with your relationship with God], then your Father will not forgive your trespasses. (AMP)

Forgiveness does not mean that you are letting that person off the hook; you are releasing them from having power over you. You benefit from forgiving yourself because it stops you from continuously condemning yourself for getting into a bad relationship. If you don't, you will always try to control every situation you are in, trying to avoid getting stuck in that place again. You do not trust your decision-making skills, so you overanalyze every little detail.

In order to move forward, I felt like God was presenting me with the opportunity to forgive my father. Even though he was dead, I knew it was time to make a choice to forgive my father and let him rest. I could no longer blame him for my actions. I had to let him go. I had to let go of that story that I used to blame and hold him responsible for every choice that I made. I decided to write my father a letter.

> Dad,
> Your inconsistency in my life hurt me deeply. For years, I have felt unloved, unwanted, and abandoned by you. All I have ever wanted from you was your love, acceptance, and validation. I thought that I had to prove that I was enough to gain your time and attention. I always

told you about my accomplishments, to show you that I was a "good kid," hoping you want to spend time with me. I would hang on to your every word because you were my dad. I would get so excited when you made plans to be with me but would be devastated when you would not show up. Dad, I just wanted you to love me. I wanted you to choose me instead of the drugs and alcohol.

I looked for your love, validation, and acceptance in men. Every boy I dated, I placed them in your position in my life. I allowed myself to be abused by a man, trying to prove that I could be loved by a man. I confused love with lust and gave myself to men, hoping they would love me back. Of course, none of those relationships worked, and those breakups made me feel abandoned.

When you came back into my life before you died, I was overjoyed. You were able to fill the voids that were there from childhood. However, you died, and those wounds reopened. Now that you are gone, I know there is nothing you can do about it.

Dad, I want you to know that I forgive you. Now that I am an adult, I understand that you loved me the best way you could and the choices you made in life had nothing to do with me. I let go of all the anger, bitterness, sadness, and narrative that I have attached to you. I no longer hold you responsible for the decisions that I make in life. I want you to rest peacefully in heaven. Dad, I love you and miss you!

Sondra~

The choices that I make from now on are not going to be from that broken place but from a healed place. It's up to me to know to do something different. It's up to me to learn self-discipline. When things began to get hard, I looked in the mirror and told myself, "I know this is hard but the past is over. I'm creating a new future for myself, trusting God and my foundation is His love for me." God loves me more than anything else.

God's unconditional love goes deeper than anything, any place, any area of my life where there are missing holes. His love goes in and covers all my wrongs. It's like sealant that you stuff in a hole on the wall, the sealant the doctor puts in your teeth for cavities. It's a replacement where there is a hole, they put the gel inside, replacing what was ruined; and all that is left is a vulnerable hole, and God says, "Now I am going to come in with my love and seal every broken and hidden place."

You have the opportunity to break that back open if you don't nurture your healed place and take care of it. The pain can come back, and God will have to resurface or reseal it again.

I started to become more aware of my feelings and the power of his love. My life was changing, and my confidence increased. I made a choice to be free and redirect the path that I was heading in—no more destruction or sadness.

I am going to try something new, I thought. *But what if I fall? Get back up! If I don't try, I will die in a place where I could have been free. God doesn't want me to die.*

John 10:10 says, "The thief comes only in order to steal and kill and destroy. I came that they may have and enjoy life, and have it in abundance [to the full, till it overflows]" (AMP). Be strong and walk in your liberty and be who God has called you to be!

I Can Do This

I returned from Oregon, encouraged, ready to face my situations that were left back in East Lansing. I was not the broken woman that left the month prior; I found Jesus and allowed Him to heal my brokenness. I felt like the woman at the well—I was ready to tell people about the man that told me everything that I ever did.

Depression, fear, shame, and domestic violence no longer had dominion over me. I didn't cower in fear when I had to speak on my past experience. I knew that wasn't a part of me anymore and I was loved by God. I'm not the only person in life who goes through tough situations.

Yes, it may have been taboo, but I was not going to let it define me. I had a new focus. It wasn't on getting a man or proving my worth to people; it was fulfilling the goal of graduating from college. During this time, I have learned how to trust the Lord with all of my heart and lean not to my own understanding.

In October 2007, I was presented with the option to either trust God or trust in myself. I heard the Lord instruct me to move to Portland, Oregon, to attend seminary after graduation. I was a senior at Michigan State University with plans to work for the Michigan State Police Forensic Lab.

At the time, God's request was not aligning with my plan that I had created for my life. I did not mind attending seminary; I always had that desire since I have been in ministry and preaching since sixteen years old. I just wanted to complete that goal later in life and in Michigan.

Leaving the place where I was born and raised, my family, and my friends to a state that I had only visited a few times was a struggle. I instantly felt like Abraham in Genesis 12. After wrapping my head around the request, I knew that I had to leave and step out on the same faith that I preached about and trust that God would work everything out.

To make a long story short, I applied and was accepted to Western Seminary (one that God guided me to), graduated from MSU in May 2008, and moved to Portland in August. By being obedient to God, I was able to find a job in forensic toxicology while working on my Masters of Divinity.

CHAPTER 4

Transition into Acceptance

Transition

I am in a place called *transition*. I am excited to be away from my past, but I am trying to set myself up to transition into my future. This is a tricky place because I cannot see what is in front of me, and I must trust God as I come into contact with different circumstances and situations. I am learning how to truly trust God wholeheartedly. I am realizing the importance of me losing control and letting God take 100 percent control of my life and leading me instead of me trying to lead God through my life so I don't experience hardships. The hardships that I was trying to avoid are the very things that are holding me back from being the woman God wants me to be. I have been living in fear and faith.

Transition is a place that we all find ourselves in at one point in our lives. This place is filled with so much anxiety because we have never experienced this journey before. The point of transition is to go from an outgrown place into new territory.

When traveling down the road of transition, there are things in our lives that need to be replaced before we can move into our new place in life. I have found that the biggest thing that needs to be changed is our mindset. In Luke 5:36–39, Jesus spoke this parable to the people:

> No one puts a piece from a new garment on an old one, otherwise the new makes a tear, and also the piece that was taken out of the new does not match the old. And no one puts new wine into old wineskins; or else the new wine will burst the wine skins and be spilled, and the wineskins will be ruined. But new wine must be put into new wineskins, and both are preserved. And no one, having drunk old wine, immediately desires new; for he says, "The old is better."

This passage explains the importance of changing our mindset before moving into a new place. God cannot allow you to bring baggage and lies of the enemy into your promise because it will ruin your promise and leave you more hurt than before. That's why it is so important to deal with the areas in your life that have held you bound. I will use myself as an example.

A few years ago, I quit my job so that I can pursue my Masters of Divinity to fulfill my dream of empowering people and helping them to live their lives more abundantly by applying the word of God into their lives. But before I came to this place, I had to deal with the insecurities that were lurking throughout my life and causing me not to trust God in every area of my life. With my mouth, I said that I trusted God; but my heart was filled with all kinds of doubt, fear, and anxiety.

During my transition, I had to learn the importance of trusting God and losing control of my life because of fear. I have found that the only reason I was so controlling was because of my fear of failing or being hurt. I knew that if I controlled every aspect of my life, I could allow only certain things in and out. What I didn't realize was that, by not trusting God to lead and direct me, I was giving the devil an open invitation into my life and why I was attracting the wrong people, things, and attitudes into my life.

I had to ask God for forgiveness and to teach me how to trust and love him so that I can live a life in accordance to his word. Once I released control and invited God into that closed area in my life,

He began to show me different areas of my life that needed to be changed. Was this process overnight? No, it is actually still occurring to this very day. I am now realizing that I am the new garment and the new wineskin, so I get a different treatment. By enduring this process, I will be able to handle the new wine (the anointing) or thread that God is using to put me back together.

Once my mind began to change, I realized that I was no longer accepting the identity given to me by the enemy; my desires, wants, and expectations began to change. God gave me the directions to follow him though the journey. He changed my mind-set so I can handle the new place in life.

A biblical example of a person who experienced a road of transition was Abraham. His transition was physical and spiritual. In Genesis 12:1–3, we find Abraham living in Haran, and the Lord speaks to him, saying,

> Get out of your country, from your family and from your father's house, to a land that I will show you. I will make your name great; and you shall be a blessing. I will bless those who bless you, and I will curse those who curse you; and in you all the families of the earth shall be blessed.

After hearing this from God, Abraham left and took his immediate family and nephew with him. From that moment, Abraham's life was in transition. The Lord gave him a glance of the outcome if he followed the instruction and commands. As you read through the next ten chapters of Genesis, you will see the process that Abraham endured to reach his new life in God. We see that he made mistakes and the process was not overnight; it actually took over twenty years for him to go from his old self (Abram) to his fulfillment (Abraham).

I will never be the same once I complete my transitional period. This part of my journey was used to show me how far I have come and that I am changing the more I surrender to God and allow God to lead me according to His will and way.

REJECTED TO ACCEPTED

I had to go back home to Michigan to go through another aspect of my journey. I have encountered some past situations that should have caught me up, but instead, I was victorious. Yes, some parts of me expected to feel the pain because that's what I grew accustomed to over the years. To go through these situations and to see my strength and trust in God prevailed made me feel so good. I learned that my life doesn't have to be controlled by hurt or pain. I no longer identify myself with my pain but with the words of God.

Just because your situation doesn't look like it is going to work out for you, continue to speak positive word of affirmation over your life and continue to focus on God. God created us before the foundation of the world, and He knows exactly what He wants and needs for your life. Matthew 6:33 says, "But seek first the kingdom of God and His righteousness and all these things shall be added to you."

The proper way to apply this scripture to your life would be when you will not allow yourself to become stressed out about who is or not in your life or how to fix your crazy situations. You are going to give the problems to God and wait until you receive the proper direction before responding. By doing this, you are keeping your focus on God and let Him fight your battles. Then will God give you the necessary tools or provision for your situation.

By taking the time to discover the way you think about yourself is life changing. For the most part, we all have an overall positive image of ourselves; and if we are doing something that we don't like, we learn how to justify our actions. I am not trying to push you into the false sense of perfection that if you fix these problem areas, you have "arrived." We will never arrive until we reach heaven.

My purpose is to expose the lies, fears, and shame the enemy has used for so long to deceive us and keep us from having healthy relationships, a positive self-image, and personal forgiveness about ourselves. For so long, I believed that I was unloved; and if I told anyone what happened to me, they would see me as damaged. The enemy used previous relationships with men, and my rejection from my father was proof that I was unloved.

As long as I believed his lies, I went into relationships thinking that I must hide my true self and decorate this false image of perfection. Instead of being who God created me to be, I was acting like a perfect (or what I thought a perfect or ideal) woman was. I would only give so much information about myself and not become emotionally connected because in three months, the man was going to get tired of me and leave.

I would start sabotaging the relationship by arguing, running away, or shutting down when my flaws or my true identity peeked out from up under my blanket of shame. Once I took some time away, I was able to tuck my flaw away and not let anyone see it again. After each relationship would end, the enemy would begin to break me down farther.

When I tell people some of the things I have experienced in life, they ask me, "How did you get over that?" My only response was "Jesus. He was my Dr. Love."

As I have stated before, my heart has been so broken repeatedly; and each time, I would say I'm not going to love anymore because love isn't working for me. Before I could finish saying that statement, I would feel my heart fill up with love, and I will hear God say, "Don't give up. I love you."

In my mind, I accepted God's love, but I really longed for natural love. I wanted a natural man to love me. God finally showed me that the love that I was craving was from my father; and since he is dead, no matter how many men I give myself to, they would never fill my dad's void. The only person that could fill that place is God.

Psalm 27:10 says, "When my mother and father forsake me, then the Lord will take care of me." Since I have been rejected so many times, I thought that God would reject me as well. He was the only one who was giving and running toward me with the love that I craved.

I was tired of giving myself to men. I prayed, "Lord, I want you to love me. I feel so used and don't believe that you can love me completely and not leave me. Every man I have ever loved has left me after they were around me for a while, so prove me wrong."

That was my last cry for help, and God answered me and said, "*Treat me like you would treat your boyfriend. Spend time getting to know me, come to me with all of your problems. When you need any-*

thing, I will supply your needs. I will give you joy for mourning, the garment of praise for the spirit of heaviness, and beauty for ashes."

Then I made up my mind that I was going to prove God wrong that He wasn't going to like me either once the truth came out. Oh, how wrong I was! The more I began to unveil all my hurts did God comfort, heal, and help me understand why my actions caused me to attract broken people. Now I know that I have someone who loves me so much.

The love that God showers on me is amazing. Each day, I learn a new aspect of him; and when I am distant, He comes and woos me again. When I am getting distracted with my personal life, He reminds me that He has a plan for me.

Chapter 5

Mirror Moments

Identifying How I See Myself

One of the most intimate places for me is in front of my mirror. My mirror sees me at my best and at my worst. My mirror is where I rehearse my sermons, give myself pep talks, reflect on my life, do my hair and makeup, and get dressed. My mirror is with me all the time.

I have two mirrors in my bedroom, two mirrors in my bathroom, and one in my purse. I'm not vain, but I do like to look at myself. Not only do I have a physical mirror, but I also have a spiritual mirror and it is used for internal checks.

For most of my life, I didn't like the woman who was on the other side of the mirror. Truthfully, I possessed low self-esteem and self-worth. When it came to my self-esteem, I didn't like how I felt about myself. I had a very low view of myself.

I was afraid and ashamed of exposing my true self to the world, so I hid behind a mask of perfection, which lead to my inauthenticity. I was unable to accept compliments. I would argue and explain why the compliment was incorrect in an agonizing fashion. I would give up easily and then beat myself up for not taking a chance, which caused me to be stuck in the past, rehearsing my past mistakes, fearing that it would cause hopelessness in my future.

Self-worth is the sense of one's value. During this time, I had no sense of value for my life. I believed I did not deserve happiness, love, peace, respect, or dignity. I wanted those things, but I didn't think I deserved them. So when I saw a spark of joy, I would be overcome with dread. I would be waiting for something bad to happen, and I would be hurt again.

I believed that my fate rested in the hands of others, leaving them with the responsibility of directing and placing the value on my life. I loved hard; I would attach my value to my affection; and when I give it to a person, I would hold on for dear life, hoping the other person would identify my worth and treat me better. I constantly compared my life to others, and I would always end up on the losing end.

This is how I felt on the inside, but on the outside, I made sure I wore my mask of perfection that made it seem like I had high self-esteem and self-worth. I made sure that I kept people at a distance because I did not want them seeing what I really looked like on the inside. It was only a select few people to whom I felt comfortable showing my flaws.

I craved having people in my inner circle, but I was too ashamed and I didn't want them to judge me for being broken. I even tried to hide this from God. I would go before Him in prayer, just as perfect as I thought I could be, like He didn't know I was being phony.

I remember going for a walk and I was praying, and the Holy Spirit said to me, "*God wants to heal your self-esteem and self-worth. You don't have to be ashamed of yourself anymore. God sees you—the real you—and He wants to heal you.*"

Tears immediately started swelling up in my eyes. I love God so much because His love never fails, and He continues to meet me and accept me just as I am. He wants me to be the best version of myself and will not allow me to be anything less than that.

The Holy Spirit continues, "*You are walking around life with a sheet covering up who you are. You dress up and put makeup on top of this sheet, hoping no one notices. When people do take notice of it and try to get close enough to peek under it, you push them away. That is not the life God has for you. Will you let Him remove the sheet so He can heal you?*"

By this time, I have made it home, and I was in tears. I realized that the more I surrendered my life to God, the more He was going to change me. I wasn't against it; I was just nervous because He wanted me. God noticed me, and I mattered to Him. My life matters to God!

I made the decision that it was time to deal with two issues that rejection intertwined in every aspect of my life. I said to the Lord, "Lord, I'm ready to deal with this. Let me know what to do, and I will do it."

Interestingly enough, nothing happened that day. I continued laying this issue before the Lord in prayer, waiting for instructions.

It was about a week later, I was looking at myself in the mirror while brushing my teeth, and the Lord asked me this question: "*Do you love yourself?*"

I stood there replaying the question, *Do I love myself?* My heart started to beat fast, "Yes, Lord, I love myself."

"*Sondra, do you really love yourself?*"

Oh boy, apparently my first answer wasn't the right one because He asked me again. It was time for me to be honest. I can't lie to the Lord; however, I didn't want to admit the truth. Who wants to say, "Lord, I am a woman in my midtwenties, and I don't love myself." I was ashamed to say this.

The Lord being gracious and compassionate comforted me with Joshua 1:9, "*Have I not commanded you? Be strong and of good courage; do not be afraid, nor be dismayed, for the Lord your God is with you wherever you go.*"

It feels good to know that Jesus is with me, no matter what happens, He will never leave me or forsake me. With a newfound confidence, I admitted the truth to the Lord and said, "Lord, I don't love myself. Please teach me how to love me."

I finished up in the bathroom, and I grabbed my journal, and the Lord instructed me to go back to the mirror and look at myself, not just my reflection but my inner self. I started to cry because I saw the things that I didn't like about myself.

"How can someone like a person like me?" I said to myself.

He then said to write down what I saw. I began identifying all the physical characteristics, character traits, and the level of my self-esteem and self-worth. I wept throughout this process because I was, for the first time, being completely honest with myself and finally getting these things off my chest.

After finishing my list, I took a second and breathed a sigh of relief. As I read through the list, some of the character traits that were written down were things that I thought I overcame.

Then God said, "*What do you like about yourself?*"

I turned my paper over and started writing the physical characteristics and character qualities that I liked about myself. Once I finished writing my list, I realized that my positive list was shorter than my negative list. No wonder I leaned more in to the negative attributes concerning my life—the negatives outweighed the positives.

Then God said to me, "*From the list of negative attributes, which ones are you struggling with the most?*"

I quickly identified feeling unlovable, rejected, fearful, and insecure. I stood before God, feeling completely vulnerable. I have exposed the areas of my life that I felt the most torment and unsure what was going to happen next.

God asked me, "*Who told you that you were these negative things?*"

This question stopped me in my tracks and reminded me of the conversation that God had with Adam in the Garden when He asked him, "*Who told you that you were naked?*"

I started thinking about that question about who told me that I was unloved, rejected, fearful, and insecure. Evidently, it was not God. That leaves two options—the devil or my past experience.

I responded, "My past." My past experiences shaped my present view of myself and the behaviors that I engaged in and tolerated from others. Just because a negative experience has happened to me, it doesn't qualify that as a truth for my life.

Lies, Fear, Shame and Truth

These are the lies that the enemy uses to hold me captive from living an abundant free life. John 10:10 says, "The thief comes only in order to steal and kill and destroy. I came that they may have and enjoy life, and have it in abundance [to the full, till it overflows]." Since the purpose of the thief is to kill, steal, and destroy, it only takes one lie to derail a person from the path that God has for them.

The definition of *lie* is "something meant to deceive"; "the manner in which something is positioned"; "to pass on false information or create a false impression." The lies from the enemy directly opposes the truths of God, with a purpose of swaying you to distrust God. By identifying the lies the enemy uses to deceive me, I will be able to withstand them.

After taking a few days to process the new information that has been uncovered in my life, I was ready to progress to the next step of identifying how I see myself. I began writing in my prayer journal, "Thank you, Lord, for showing me lies that the enemy uses to hold me captive. I am ready to uncover more information. What should I do next?"

I went on to spend some time reading my Bible and worshipping. I decided to revisit the list of lies the enemy uses against me. And then the question came to me, *What are you afraid will happen if these things were to happen?*

Lies	Fear
Unlovable	I will never get married and experience a healthy relationship with a man.
Rejected	I will remain emotionally unavailable, not being able to fully trust or depend on people.
Fearful	I will be exposed as a fraud for not being as strong or "perfect" as I portray myself to be.
Insecure	I will never be content with my looks, personality, and life.

For the first time, I see how the lies and the fears work together to kept me defeated and away from what God has for me. As I was going through this experience, different scriptures were beginning to make more sense to me, especially the role of the Spirit in John 14:16–17:

> And I will ask the Father, and He will give you another Helper (Comforter, Advocate, Intercessor—Counselor, Strengthener, Standby), to be with you forever—the Spirit of Truth, whom the world cannot receive [and take to its heart] because it does not see Him or know Him, but you know Him because He (the Holy Spirit) remains with you continually and will be in you.

The Holy Spirit was really operating within the roles of a comforter, advocate, intercessor, counselor, strengthener, and standby for me; and I am so grateful. God is so real and will help you overcome any situation or circumstance that keeps you from living the life He has for you.

The next thing I needed to identify was the shame that caused the fear and was birthed from the lie. *Shame* is defined as a "sense of guilt or unworthiness; disgrace or humiliation; a disappointment." The next question was, *What happened to cause you to feel guilty or unworthy?*

Lies	Fear	Shame
Negative attribute	Afraid is going to happen	Event that caused guilt
Unlovable	I will never get married and experience a healthy relationship with a man.	I had sex before marriage and the relationship didn't work.
Rejected	I will remain emotionally unavailable, not being able to fully trust or depend on people.	My father wasn't consistently in my life. I had to initiate a relationship with him, or we wouldn't have one.

Fearful	I will be exposed as a fraud for not being as strong or perfect as I portray to be.	When I shared my wounds, disappointments, fears, or failures, I would receive a critical response.
Insecure	I will never be content with my looks, personality, and life.	I was teased as a child for being short and dark skinned. I didn't receive the affirmation I needed.

I am grateful that even when I exposed the depths of my heart to God, He reinforces His love for me. God was not surprised that I believed these things; He wanted to know if I trusted Him enough to give Him the lies in exchange for His truth. I was then instructed to find scriptures that would contrast the lies.

In order to know God's perspective, I needed to use the Bible since

> all Scripture is God-breathed [given by divine inspiration] and is profitable for instruction, for conviction [of sin], for correction [of error and restoration to obedience], for training in righteousness [learning to live in conformity to God's will, both publicly and privately—behaving honorably with personal integrity and moral courage]; so that the man of God may be complete and proficient, outfitted and thoroughly equipped for every good work. (2 Tim. 3:16–17)

Once I found the scriptures that directly contrasted the lies, I had to rehearse those truth statements every day until I begin to believe them in my heart and mind. I placed them on all of my mirrors, and every time I saw my reflection, I would repeat them.

REJECTED TO ACCEPTED

Lies	Fear	Shame	Truth
Unlovable	I will never get married and experience a healthy relationship with a man.	I had sex before marriage, and the relationship didn't work.	Nor height nor depth, nor anything else in all creation will *be able to separate us from the love of God* which is in Christ Jesus our Lord. (Rom. 8:39, emphasis mine) The Lord appeared from of old to me, saying, Yes, *I have loved you with an everlasting love*; therefore with loving-kindness have I drawn you and continued My faithfulness to you. (Jer. 31:3, emphasis mine)
Rejected	I will remain emotionally unavailable, not being able to fully trust or depend on people.	My father wasn't consistently in my life. I had to initiate a relationship with him, or we wouldn't have one.	For you have not received a spirit of slavery leading again to fear [of God's judgment], *but you have received the Spirit of adoption* as sons [the Spirit producing sonship] by which we [joyfully] cry, "Abba! Father!" (Rom. 8:15, emphasis mine) Although my father and my mother have abandoned me, *yet the Lord will take me up [adopt me as His child]*. (Ps. 27:10, emphasis mine)

Fearful	I will be exposed as a fraud for not being as strong or perfect as I portray to be.	When I shared my wounds, disappointments, fears, or failures, I was would receive a critical response.	For God did not give us a spirit of timidity or cowardice or fear, but *[He has given us a spirit] of power and of love and of sound judgment and personal discipline* [abilities that result in a calm, well-balanced mind and self-control]. (2 Tim. 1:7, emphasis mine) "Be strong and courageous. *Do not be afraid; do not be discouraged for the Lord your God is with you* wherever you go." (Josh. 1:9, emphasis mine)
Insecure	I will never be content with my looks, personality, and life.	I was teased as a child for being short and dark skinned. I didn't receive the affirmation I needed.	She *opens her mouth with wisdom, and the teaching of kindness is on her tongue.* (Prov. 31:26, emphasis mine) You are *beautiful for you are fearfully and wonderfully made*. (Ps. 139:14, emphasis mine) "For *I know the plans and thoughts that I have for you,*" says the Lord, "*plans for peace and well-being and not for disaster,* to *give you a future and a hope.*" (Jer. 29:11, emphasis mine)

Be Free!

By the time I was done with this exercise, I was sobbing. I had been carrying this for a long time. My identity was being changed; I was exposing my truth to God while getting healed at the same time.

"Free" by Kierra Sheard was playing in the background of my apartment. I love gospel music because it allows me to create an environment of praise and worship in my home. It had to be a God moment because right as I was surrendering all these things to God, Kierra starts declaring,

> Where the spirit of the Lord our God is at rest there is freedom, you can be free from bondage and healed from brokenness and full of joy be free. Be free! Be free! Be free from the bitterness in your heart! Be free from the dysfunctional relationships, you can be free from bondage and healed from brokenness and full of joy be free. Be free from whatever mommy or daddy did to you! Be free from whatever it is that you went through behind closed doors. You can be free from, bondage and healed from, you just have to believe it! Be Free from whatever demon it is that you are wrestling with! I decree and I declare it in the name of Jesus, you can be free from whatever it is you're going through, the mind games, the mind games. I speak Jesus, the blood of Jesus against it. I come against the with the blood of Jesus, you have to pass over. I speak freedom in the atmosphere! Be Free, Be free! Lift your hands if you want to be free, if you receive that you are free. I come against witch, warlock, every demon that is not like God. I come against every force that is not like the God Almighty that I serve. I speak the blood of Jesus against every attack, against every plan, against every spirit that is not

like God. For he has given us the power. He has not given us the spirit of fear but of *power* and love and of a sound, I *got a sound mind*. It doesn't matter what I'm going through, I'm Free!

It was like she was speaking directly to me. I could be free from the bondage of low self-esteem and self-worth, sadness, rejection, all the lies, fears, and the shame from which I shaped my dysfunctional identity. As I lay on the ground before the Lord, I could feel the presence of God all over me. It felt like strength was being imparted into my body, and the more I cried, the more the brokenness was removed.

I kept on praising God until I got tired. Once I finished, I felt so much lighter. It was as if a huge weight was off my shoulders and I could breathe easy. I went to look at myself in the mirror, and my eyes were puffy but didn't mind; I saw myself differently. I liked the person that I saw, and I wanted to introduce her to the world. Before I could do that, I needed to encourage myself.

What Are You Thinking About?

In order to maintain this new perspective, I had to change my mind-set concerning the way that I see myself. Changing your mind-set is a continuous process that allows for constant growth in your spiritual and natural life. That's why Romans 12:2 instructs us,

> Do not be conformed to this world (this age), [fashioned after and adapted to its external, superficial customs], *but be transformed (changed) by the [entire] renewal of your mind* [by its new ideals and its new attitude], so that you may prove [for yourselves] what is the good and acceptable and perfect will of God, even the thing which is good and acceptable and perfect [in His sight for you].

It's imperative that I embraced the mind of Christ because I relied on past personal experiences to understand life rather than what God said. Since I had a bad experience with love, I thought that I was unlovable or incapable of loving people. I had to understand that my identity is not what I have experienced; rather, my identity is found in who Christ says that I am.

It is impossible for a person to consistently behave in a way that is inconsistent with their character. Moreover, negative thoughts will cause me to produce a "'they' syndrome." This syndrome is based in fear and shifts my focus to what people will think about me—"What will they say, what will they think, what will they do?" Now you can't live for yourself; you are living for a "they" that doesn't exist. How many "theys" do we have that are holding our lives captive?

By taking on a renewed mind, I was given the ability to take my thoughts under subjection. Second Corinthians 10:4–5 says,

> For the weapons of our warfare are not physical [weapons of flesh and blood], but they are mighty before God for the overthrow and destruction of strongholds, [Inasmuch as we] *refute arguments and theories and reasonings and every proud and lofty thing that sets itself up against the [true] knowledge of God; and we lead every thought and purpose away captive into the obedience of Christ* [italics mine] (the Messiah, the Anointed One).

I have the power and the authority to stop myself from thinking negative thoughts and change them into positive thoughts. Philippians 4:8 explains the kind of positive thoughts I should think on:

> Finally, believers, whatever is *true*, whatever is *honorable* and *worthy of respect*, whatever is *right* and *confirmed by God's word*, whatever is *pure and wholesome*, whatever is *lovely* and *brings peace*, whatever is *admirable and of good repute*; if there is any *excellence*, if there is *anything worthy of praise, think continually on these things* [center

your mind on them, and implant them in your heart]. (Italics mine)

When a negative thought comes to my mind, I can use the truth statements from the Lies, Fear, Shame, and Truth exercise—*Why did you say that? That was so dumb?* I can bring that thought under subjection by saying, "That's a lie. When I speak, I open my mouth with wisdom, and the teaching of kindness is on my tongue." I am stopping that lie right in its tracks.

Put on the Armor of God

As I reflect on my journey of identifying the lies, fear, and shame that shaped the negative outlook that I had on myself and the process of embracing the truth of who I am from God's perspective, in order to keep this positive mind-set, the armor of God is essential.

The armor of God is composed of seven different parts: the belt of truth, the shield of faith, the breastplate of righteousness, the helmet of salvation, the shoes of peace, the sword of the spirit, and the prayer that are used to explain the purpose and the importance of utilizing different aspects of righteousness. The armor of God is discussed in Ephesians 6:10–18, and it is what helps that

> You may be able to [successfully] stand against all the *schemes* and *the strategies and the deceits of the devil.* For our struggle is not against flesh and blood [contending only with physical opponents], but against the rulers, against the powers, against the world forces of this [present] darkness, against the spiritual forces of wickedness in the heavenly (supernatural) places. Therefore, put on the complete armor of God, so that you will be able to [successfully] resist and stand your ground in the evil day [of danger], and having done everything [that the crisis demands], to

stand firm [in your place, fully prepared, immovable, victorious]. (Eph. 6:11–13, italics mine)

I am relieved to know that I no longer have to defend myself in our own strength but I have an awesome power available to operate in. The schemes, devices, and deceits mentioned in the scriptures are the negative thoughts, insecurities, rejection, and humiliation these are the things the enemy uses to hold me captive. There will be times when the battle may become intense, but I refuse to retreat—I will *stand firm*.

What does the armor of God look like? The Amplified Bible gives a very detailed explanation:

- *Belt of truth.* Personal integrity, moral courage around your waist.
- *Breastplate of righteousness.* An upright heart.
- *Shoes of peace.* Prepared to face the enemy with firm-footed stability and the readiness produced by the good news.
- *Shield of faith.* Protective—with which you can extinguish all the flaming arrows of the evil one.
- *Helmet of salvation.* Knowledge of God's salvation and love for you.
- *Sword of the spirit.* which is the Word of God.
- *Prayer.* With specific requests or petitions at all times.

Prayer

Lord, I thank you for revealing to me the things that I have believed about myself. I am asking for forgiveness for believing the lies, fear, and shame of the enemy. I surrender my mind, heart, will, and emotions over to you.

Help me to change my way of thinking so I can begin to see myself being victorious and not a victim. I trust you with all my heart and believe what you think about me. Open my eyes so that I can see myself the way that you see me. Let it be easy for me to speak positive, encouraging, and loving words to myself each time I see my reflection. I pray for the scriptures that I use as truth statements to be brought back to my memory when negative thoughts come to my mind.

I thank you for your unfailing, unconditional, and never-failing love for me. I pray for courage to love myself the way you love me. Thank you for filling all of the voids of my life. Continue to walk with me through this journey and give me the strength to create new habits in my life.

Lord, I need the courage to reveal these things to my accountability partner. I have privately worked through this. I know I need to share this experience publicly so that I can have someone hold me accountable. In Jesus's name, amen.

Accountability Partner

It took about three days for me to contact my accountability partner, but once I did, I had an amazing breakthrough. Before we started discussing the lies, fear, and shame that I was dealing with, I felt so uneasy. I could hear the enemy filling my mind with more lies like, "If you tell her this list, she will think that you are a fraud. You are not as holy as you thought you were."

Once I heard that, I knew that I had to expose the enemy for who he was. When I told Marla the lies, fear, and shame that I dealt with, she immediately spoke the word of God over my life and she affirmed who I was as a woman of God.

Each time we met with each other, we began to dig deep into my life and figure out where the lies began. I have found that all lies come from a truth moment. I also realized that the lies, fear, and shame built upon each other. Once we started breaking down the situations, I was able to forgive myself for allowing myself to engage in those hurtful and unhealthy situations.

Once I forgave myself, I wanted to go out and tell everyone I knew about dealing with the lies, fear, and shame in their lives. For me, it felt like I was having a woman at the well in John 4. My heart's desire is for everyone to experience the freedom and forgiveness that I have gained through this exercise.

After meetings with my accountability partner, I thought it would be a great idea to incorporate the Lies, Fear, and Shame exercise into my personal devotional time. Since the Lord has exposed the enemy's lies in my life, I must keep myself before the Lord. First Peter 5:8 says, "Be sober, be vigilant; because your adversary the devil walks about like a roaring lion, seeking whom he may devour."

By praying, reading my Bible, and asking the Lord to strengthen the areas that are weak in my life, I must continue to develop my relationship with Christ on a daily basis so that I can live a healthy life and able to minister effectively. I also say this mantra aloud every day: "I am beautiful, I am important, and I am loved." This mantra covers three of the areas the lies came from. I can always revert to the positive and uplifting words that I have read in my devotional time to encourage me throughout the day.

Chapter 6

Accepting Who I Am

You Are Enough

You are enough! There is nothing that is hidden from you. There is nothing that is taken from you. You are awesome, you are wonderful, you are enough! You don't have to prove your worth. You don't have to work hard so that people will like you. You don't have to be perfect; you don't have to forget your truth for someone else. You don't have to do that, you don't.

I know it is so hard because you want people to like you, and you want the thing that you haven't had and you're willing to do whatever it takes to get it. But, baby, I want you to know that you don't have to do that. If you have not received the thing that you desire, it does not mean that you will not receive it. It is imperative that you do not become obsessed with this desire that you allow it to define who you are.

Being married doesn't define you or give you more clout; it doesn't give you more love or acceptance. Your value isn't found in your marital status, bank account, employment, or social involvement. Your value comes from known who you are, what you bring to the world, knowing that God loves you, and has a plan for your life. So every day you wake up you are focused on fulfilling the destiny that is on the inside of you.

When God sent Moses back to Egypt in Gen. 4. Moses was instructed to use the rod that was in his hand to prove that God had sent him on this assignment. Every time Moses needed to perform a miracle he used what was in his hand. He did not need to utilize anything outside of himself to fulfill the plan God had for his life. It's the same for you. Everything that you need is in your hands. The purpose that you are looking for is in your hands. The love that you are looking for is in your hands. It's in your hands.

At times, we want other people to validate what we are doing in order to believe that we are in the right direction, and sometimes we just have to believe in ourselves. You have to be your own cheerleader. You have to, and that's okay. It is absolutely okay to be your own cheerleader and say, "If nobody else believes in you, I believe in you. If no one else says 'I love you,' know that I love you." If nobody else gets behind your vision, you get behind your vision. You have to love yourself enough to know that everything that your hand touches will be gold.

By believing in yourself and having God's love on the inside, gives you the ability to do impossible things. You will be able to give and receive love, to be nice, caring, to succeed, and to live a healthy full life. Most importantly, you will be able truthfully quote Philippians 4:13, "I can do all things through Christ who strengthens me."

It also means that we have to silence the past. Yes, our past molds who we are, but it does not have the power to shape our future. Those situations in your life were things that can be used to change your life. Yes, it could set you on a path of destruction, or it could set you on the path to success.

If you look at Joseph's life (Genesis chapters 37, 39-45), he was given a very bad hand all throughout his life, he had family issues, was sold into slavery, he lived in a country he didn't know anything about, and was sent to prison for a crime he didn't commit. It was not until he was thirty did things turn around for him.

With all of his shortcomings, Joseph was still able to live into his fullness. His integrity remained intact when he thought no one was watching. He believed in himself when no one else believed in him. Even though he was in prison he made the most of the situation. Internally he knew that he was enough in both the prison and the palace. It is important for you to accept that you are enough! You are enough at work with your children, with your friends, with your family, or at church. Go ahead and write a book, get a new job, or even go back to school. There is nothing in you that you can't do.

You have to believe in yourself. Sometimes it's not the devil telling you that you can't do it; it's you telling yourself that you can't do it. You talk yourself right out of whatever it is that you want or whatever it is that you need because you focus on the negative.

It's so important to change that mentality and to walk into the light of love and allow things to happen. Everything is not governed by fear or abandonment. My mom has always told me that "rejection is God's protection"; and when God removes something from your life, it is to protect you.

Maybe your heart is ready to be in a relationship. But what are you bringing to the table? If a man shows up to your life, what are you capable of doing emotionally, based on the state that you are in at the moment?

We think that this person is going to change us, but the same insecurity you have now is going to be the same insecurity when they are there, except it will be maximized because you are expecting for this person to make you completely happy. You are still going to be miserable because he or she is not jumping through fifty thousand hoops to make you feel wanted or validating his or her love for you. That's going to be an issue—you're going to always question his or her love, you're going to always want to know if you are enough.

If he or she is not calling enough, laughing enough, saying thank you enough, or stroking your ego enough, it's the core of who you are that has to change. Your viewpoint has to change. The way that you see life has to change. No one is going to change that but you.

That's when you have to start doing the work. For me, it took me a long time and is still taking me some time to really embrace that I am enough. There are times when I am like, "I am enough, I am good." But then there are times when I am feeling nervous or unsure.

In these moments, I pray, "Lord, show me that I am enough. Let me be enough." I felt like the man who was at the pool of Bethesda for thirty-eight years. I have been given the choice to either live a full life or stay there in my brokenness. I have to have the courage to stand up and walk.

Like the man at the pool of Bethesda, he didn't have the strength to walk. He didn't know how to walk; he had been there for thirty-eight years. When Jesus said, "Will you be made whole? Then pick up your mat and follow me," he saw other people around him walking and he did what he saw. He made a choice and got up and started walking.

That's what I need to do—just get up, pick up my mat, and start walking toward Jesus. Now that I am walking, I no longer need the mat. I can use the mat as a testimony whereas before your mat was your crutch.

You have the authority and ability to silence those negative thoughts. Sometimes, those negative thoughts become comfort; and all you know is negative and what you expect is negative. It's time to stop thinking like that.

Sing a new song, get a new narrative, read a new book. You can do it. The book that you are reading is only holding you back. The thing that you believe is the only thing holding you back. Matthew 11:28–30 says, "Come unto me all you who are weary and heavy laden and I will give you rest. Take my yolk upon you and learn of me for my yolk is easy and my burden is light." Jesus is saying in this passage, "I'm willing to exchange everything that you are going through, all of your pain, for something lighter." When you take on His yolk, all He needs from you is your obedience. That's it!

Be obedient and when times get tough, put on the armor. The Lord has you covered. He covers your head, your heart, your feet, your mind, and everything on you. God even gives you a sword and a shield. He's got you; He only requests your obedience. Your obedience is attached to helping God fulfill His plan on the earth.

Since He gave dominion to man to rule and reign, He has to use you as His mouthpiece. And it's not just in the pulpit or at the church house, but He has called you to go into the workplace, into the world, and speak and be His hands and feet. Your obedience unlocks this truth unto so many people. It is bigger than you. Sometimes we get stuck in our own worlds, and all we see is us and what we want and how we need it for ourselves. It shows those who were once a part of the faith who gave up that Christ is real.

You are called, you are chosen, and greatness lives inside you. What greatness is inside you? Jesus Christ is inside you. That's why the scripture says, "Greater is HE who is in me, than he who is in the world" (1 John 4:4). There is a song that says, "Through you I can do anything, I can do all things, cause it's you who gives me strength, nothing is impossible."

God just needs your obedience to believe that you are enough. It proves to the spirit realm that you can, through Christ, overcome the enemy, the distractions, the sin nature and that you can do anything. You are capable of doing anything that you put your mind to.

God is bigger than your struggle. He is bigger, greater, and stronger than what you see and what you are experiencing. You just have to dial into who's inside you. If you are not sure who is inside you because you don't know Him, let me introduce you to Him—His name is Jesus Christ. He died for you over two thousand years ago on the cross of Calvary for the forgiveness of your sins.

Jesus thought so much of you that He wrapped himself in humanity, laid aside some of his divinity, and came into the earth for thirty-three years. He saw it all, experienced it all, understood emotional hardships, and then died a brutal death that you deserved. But He stood in your place. Three days later, He rose with all power in His hands. He did all of that because you are loved, and His love for you is more than you can ever imagine.

You don't have to know it all or understand the plan all the way—just do what He is asking you to do. Seek Him for direction. If He is asking you to do something, stay at his feet. You go and press into His presence. You have to look for Him and believe that He loves you, and He is big enough to help you.

He has your world in His hand, and when your world and His world collides, greatness will come out of it. Let this rest in you. Let the truth of God's word and His acknowledgment of who you are.

Let that be what fights for you. Let that be the oil that cleanses you, the water that washes over you and cleanses you and erases those negative things and pushes them aside, as you surrender them over and you break your alabaster box before Him.

You are releasing all those anxieties, fears, insecurities, and failures while saying, "God, I'm giving it all to you. I withhold nothing from you. My hands are open, lifted up, and outstretched. I am letting go of fear. I don't want to be driven by fear anymore. I want to live in faith. I want to believe, no longer afraid.

"Here I am, wash my heart, wash my mind, forgive me, God. I repent, I want to change my ways. Show me the way that I need to go. Give me the courage to believe that I am enough, the wisdom to walk in the truth of your word, and in obedience to the assignment you gave me.

"I thank you for letting me know that you see me and you hear me. I thank you, Lord God, that you wrap your arms around me and tell me that you love me and that you will never leave me or forsake me. I thank you for being more than enough for me. I thank you, Lord, for showing me the truth and taking the scales off my eyes, for giving me the courage to stand up and walk.

"You can talk to anyone else, you can heal anyone else, yet you came down to me and you wanted to touch my heart. God, I thank you, and I count it as a privilege and an honor that you want to speak with me. Use me for your glory and not just in this moment, oh God, but in all moments.

"I will be obedient in all that you ask me to do. I will not grow stagnant but will remember your goodness, love, and word and will meditate on it day and night so that I might not sin against you. I will let your word be the lamp unto my feet and the light unto my pathways. I will trust you with my whole heart and acknowledge you in all my ways. I will allow you to purify my heart and change my mind. I will step out of perfection and walk in excellence to do all that you are asking of me. In Jesus's name."

Chapter 7

Accepting My Past

Just when I thought that I put the whole issue of domestic violence behind me, it reemerged in the seminary. I took a class that focused on shepherding women who had experienced traumatic experiences. Sure enough, domestic violence was an issue discussed.

As the guest speaker was lecturing, it felt like she was telling my story to the class. I sat through the lecture with so many thoughts running through my mind. A part of me wanted to run out of the room and not listen anymore. The other half of me wanted to stay and face the information head on. I was confused because my emotions were all over the place, even though I thought I had dealt with my feelings from my abusive relationship.

I left class that day with a ton of questions for myself. I wondered if I was really healed or not. Was the progress I had made all for nothing? Maybe there was something left from my past relationship that I hadn't even thought about dealing with.

I decided to pray about the matter and release it to God. I realized that in order to be completely free from that situation, I needed to confront the emotions that were surfacing. I have come to understand that I can receive healing on a specific issue multiple times. Since something like domestic violence impacted every aspect of my life, I needed each of those parts rebuilt at the pace that I can handle. It wasn't until the next semester that I would get enough courage to contact ARMS (Abuse Recovery Ministry & Services). This was the

Christian organization that our guest lecturer was from. I was in need of an internship, so why not complete two assignments at once, one for school and the other personal healing?

For one of my responsibilities as an intern was to attend Her Journey. Her Journey was the fifteen-week support group for women who have experienced domestic violence. This group met once a week for an hour. It wasn't like a standard support group where each person gets a turn to tell their story.

The leader has fifteen different lessons that varies from understanding domestic violence, setting healthy boundaries, forgiveness, self-care, and anger, with each lesson grounded in God's Word. They gave a little time for women to share their stories, asked for prayer requests, and we left. At the end of each lesson, there were homework assignments that we could do if we wanted, but were not required.

I sat in each class, fighting back tears because I was receiving so much clarity on aspects of my life and how I ended up in that situation. I came to the conclusion that I still had residue left on me from that relationship, even though I was out of it for six years. This class did an amazing job at explaining the different stages that women mentally go through because of the relationship and how to conquer the fear of getting back into that kind of relationship again.

Each lesson pointed me toward God's love and the importance of receiving his love. For me, the class confirmed the journey of healing and self-discovery God had walked me through years prior was Him. I wasn't making this stuff up. He was with me, leading me and guiding me into all truth.

I am so grateful for this experience! I had never been a part of a support group before, and it brought so much relief to me. I had a hard time connecting with people when I discuss my domestic violence experience because people would not and could not understand why I would stay in that type of relationship. They would offer their opinion having never experienced anything like that before, and it would come off as judgmental.

However, going to a support group, I was around other women who experienced similar things as I did; and it removed the lie that I was alone and no one would understand my journey. During our time together, we would laugh, cry, encourage, and pray for one another. It was a safe environment that was needed for authentic healing to occur.

Once my semester came to an end, I couldn't thank ARMS enough for not only allowing me to fulfill my internship requirements but also experience my personal growth and healing as well. I decided to finish my last three semesters of internship with them in addition to taking on a job with the organization. I had the privilege of becoming a facilitator for the Her Journey program. This opportunity was another confirmation of my ministry calling to help hurting women reach their full potential in Christ. I knew that I could do this; and I have received the necessary training from seminary, ministry, and this program to fulfill this call in the realm of domestic violence.

I had to mentally prepare myself before teaching each week. To me, I felt like each class was like a Bible study, and since I was the leader, I would be like a pastor because I had to provide pastoral care to the women and teach the lesson with compassion and carefulness. I love being able to help the women by providing them hope through the lesson, allowing them to process their current emotions without trying to fix it and being able to show compassion to the women.

The most enjoyable thing I have learned about the women I had ministered to is their transformation story. When abused women begin attending Her Journey classes, they are broken down, hurting, and ashamed. As they start to embrace the lessons that are taught and apply the tools given to their lives, each week, I watch them become stronger emotionally, find their voices, and understand God's love for them.

I had one lady share her story with me, and she said that she was unsure how she was going to make it because her identity was wrapped into her abuser. A month later, she updated me on her life, and she was excited to tell me that she has been finding identity and enjoying the time she spends discovering new things that she likes to do. That really encouraged me because I am given the opportunity to see God restore the lives of people who thought it could never happen.

The most difficult thing I have learned about the women I have ministered to is their abusive history. Each time I sit with an abused woman, I have to prepare myself to listen to their story. Some of the information that is shared with me is so hurtful and makes my heart ache.

At times, I wonder how they survived those relationships, but then I am reminded of God's protection. Since abuse is not just physical but includes verbal, emotional, psychological, spiritual, financial, and animal; different women come with questions at need to be answered about their abuser and why they do such horrible things. I now understand the importance of not trying to fix every situation and allowing the women to vent and process through their situations.

I have found the ladies in my Her Journey class to be more responsive to the rhetorical questions that provided in each lesson. While we lay the groundwork to help build their self-esteem, we also ask questions that will cause them to critically think about their situation and cause them to reflect on situations that were not so apparent to be unhealthy. During a lesson, I will have a woman receive an aha moment, and she shares it and we take a few minutes and process through it. This process is beneficial because it allows the women to reach within themselves for answers and not depend on others for an opinion.

Understanding Why I Experienced Domestic Abuse

Ever since my abusive relationship in 2006, I always wondered, *Why did I have to go through that experience? Did I do something to deserve that kind of treatment?* I finally received my answer while I was facilitating my Her Journey class, and I realized that I was called to a specific group of women and I would have never understood their perspective or be willing to have the amount of compassion that I do, had I not experienced domestic violence myself. It was bigger than just me.

God was using my life and my experience to encourage other women to know that no matter what you have experienced, God loves you and He will never leave you nor forsake you. Your life is not over because you have experienced hardship. If you are still living, there is a plan for your life. It is not over; your life is just beginning! *You can begin again!* With Jesus, all things are possible.

It reminds me of the story of Joseph in the Book of Genesis. He went through so many things that he didn't deserve and was unjustly treated, but, in the end, God turned everything around and gave him the ability to save his family as well as the nations of people from starvation. The process may not be easy, but God has equipped you with the strength to endure your process of healing. When the time is right, you will get your chance to impart life into others through your story.

Questions Concerning Domestic Violence

I worked in the world of domestic violence for three years, and during that time, I received a plethora of questions concerning domestic violence. I wanted to provide clarity on different aspects and specific questions that are presented in the world of domestic abuse. I will say this: domestic violence is one of the hardest topics to discuss because it is multifaceted and is surrounded by guilt and shame.

In this section, I will define domestic abuse, types of abuse; I will answer questions; how someone gets involved in domestic abuse; why they stay; how to support someone involved in this situation; and tools for helping people overcome.

What Is Domestic Abuse?

Domestic abuse/violence is defined as "a pattern of abusive behavior in any relationship that is used by one partner to gain or maintain power and control over another intimate partner. This includes any behaviors that intimidate, manipulate, humiliate, isolate, frighten, terrorize, coerce, threaten, blame, hurt, injure, or wound someone" (US Department of Justice). Domestic abuse can be expressed in a variety of ways, according to the US Department of Justice:

Types of Abuse

1. *Physical.* Hitting, slapping, shoving, grabbing, pinching, biting, hair pulling, etc. This type of abuse also includes denying a partner medical care or forcing alcohol and/or drug use upon him or her.
2. *Psychological/Emotional.* Causing fear by intimidation; threatening physical harm to self, partner, children, or partner's family or friends; destruction of pets and property; and forcing isolation from family, friends, or school and/or work.
    a) *Emotional.* Undermining an individual's sense of self-worth and/or self-esteem is abusive. This may include but is not limited to constant criticism, diminishing one's abilities, name-calling, or damaging one's relationship with his or her children
3. *Verbal.* Put-downs, name-calling, shouting, swearing, abusive jokes, threats, the silent treatment, continual arguing, belittling, controlling conversations, countering or discounting, criticizing, or blaming.
4. *Sexual.* Coercing or attempting to coerce any sexual contact or behavior without consent. Sexual abuse includes but is certainly not limited to marital rape, attacks on sexual parts of the body, forcing sex after physical violence has occurred, or treating one in a sexually demeaning manner.
5. *Financial.* This is defined as making or attempting to make an individual financially dependent by maintaining total control over financial resources, withholding one's access to money, or forbidding one's attendance at school or employment.
6. *Spiritual.* Misusing scriptures or God to control or abuse, negatively affecting someone's image of self or God, demanding submission and obedience, questioning her salvation, or not letting her go or making her go to church.
7. *Property.* Punching walls or doors, kicking or hitting furniture, throwing things, destroying things, slamming doors,

pounding tables, sabotaging cars, destroying cell phones, or pulling cords out of the wall.
8. *Animal.* Kicking the dog, throwing the cat, harming or killing an animal, threatening to get rid of a family pet, neglect, not feeding or watering your pet, or throwing things at an animal.

How Does Someone Get Involved in Domestic Abuse?

Abuse does not just happen; it is a learned behavior. You can learn to either give it or receive it. Since domestic abuse is about power and control, it is not specific to a certain sociological class, ethnicity, gender, religion, sexual orientation, or lifestyle—anybody can find themselves in this type of relationship for multiple reasons. A few of those reasons could include unmet childhood needs, experienced a trauma or abuse, possess low self-esteem and low self-worth, have a "fix it" mentality, or are attracted to an emotionally unavailable man.

Unmet childhood needs. This person is looking for love, acceptance, and validation from a parent. From the time a child is born, there is an immediate longing for the love and acceptance from their parents. As the bonds between child and parent continue to grow, an awareness of self-assurance and trust in that child begins to develop.

The relationship that is established between parents and children begins as an infant, molded during adolescences, and tested during the teenage years. The time that a child spends with their father during the formative years, whether healthy or unhealthy, will be the pattern that is recreated in future relationships. If a child does not receive either love, acceptance, or validation, it will cause a void in their heart and will begin to look for love in all of the wrong places.

Experienced a trauma or abuse. This is a person who had to endure a very devastating circumstance that affected them emotionally. It could have been the death of a parent, sibling, close relative or family friend, parent's divorce, being violated by a trusted person, being abused, or living with a critical parent. A critical parent is one who always finds a reason when the child does something wrong or how they could improve. Experiencing an emotional trauma can cause a person to stop maturing emotionally. If a trauma happened at thirteen years old and was never addressed at thirty years old when presented with a complicated situation that triggers an emotional reaction, the response will be that of a teenager instead of an adult.

Has low self-esteem. Self-esteem is the way a person feels about themselves. If a person is exhibiting low self-esteem, they have a low or poor view of themselves. They are afraid and ashamed of exposing their true selves to the world, so they hide behind masks of perfection, which leads to inauthenticity.

They are unable to accept praise. They argue and explain why the praise was incorrect in an agonizing fashion. This person gives up easily and never stands up for themselves, which causes them to be stuck in the past, regretting their past mistakes, fearing that it will cause hopelessness in their future.

Has low self-worth. Self-worth is the sense of one's value. If a person is exhibiting low self-worth, they have no sense of value for their lives. They believe they do not deserve happiness, love, peace, respect, or dignity. When they see a spark of joy, they are overcome with dread. They believe that their fate rests in the hands of others, leaving them with the responsibility of directing and placing the value on their lives.

This person loves hard. They attach their value to their affection, and when they give it to a person, they hold on for dear life, hoping the other person will identify their worth and treat them better. This person constantly compares their lives to others and always losses.

Has a "fix it" mentality. This is the person who always takes on the role of counselor to their family members and friends. They are attracted to people who have great potential to be awesome but need a little work. They take them on as a "project" and try to fix them.

They utilize their nurturing abilities to help build people to find and embrace their worth. They possess the remedy for everyone else's problems so they can avoid their own problems and situations. This person always wonders why people leave them after they have spent all their time investing in their well-being. This is also called the *messiah complex*.

Attracted to the emotionally unavailable man. An emotionally unavailable man is the "man of mystery" or has the "bad boy" image. He is unable to fully connect with a person emotionally. They tend to keep you at arm's length when it comes to their personal lives. This is the person who intrigues you and makes you want to figure them out.

This person is a charmer. They will tell you everything that you want to hear but rarely delivering on those promises. They possess a limited amount of affection. This person starts out a relationship showing a lot of affection, but things begin to take a turn and they stop showing any type of affection.

They prefer to become sexually familiar rather quickly. They would rather focus on being sexually intimate than emotionally intimate. They possess an elusive conduct. They are only available when it is convenient for them. They disappear for long periods of time with no regular contact and come back like nothing happened. Their words and actions are not congruent. They can tell you they love you but act in unloving ways.

The reasons highlighted above directly affect the way a person views themselves, which correlates to the kind of person that they subconsciously believe that they deserve. Since domestic abuse is about power and control, the abuser will prey on or be attracted to people with these characteristics because they are desperate for love, validation, and a relationship. The abuser will present themselves as the knight in shining armor—being nice and attentive, sweeping them off their feet, telling them what you want to hear, being the rescuer, and basically filling the void that is present in their life. The purpose is to gain their trust so they can control how they can give or take their love away. The abuser will slowly start using a combination of the types of abuse to break down the remaining self-esteem and self-worth of the person in order keep them in the relationship.

Why Does Someone Stay in an Abusive Relationship?

A person never volunteers to be in a relationship that has domestic abuse present. The situation is completely different than a normal relationship's conflict, so the mind-set of this type of relationship is downright unhealthy. The motive behind the relationship from both parties are unrealistic. The motive for the abuser is power and control, and the motive for the person is to have their voids filled. A person involved in this kind of relationship can stay for a variety of reasons. Some include being afraid, thinking they can change the abuser, have lost their identity, they don't think they deserve anything better, don't have an exit plan, and they love their partner.

Being afraid. This is a person who has experienced the wrath of their abuser, and they do not have the courage to resist the treatment they have receiving. They believe that their life or the lives of those closest to them are in jeopardy. They do not see a safe way out of the relationship, which makes them endure the abuse to protect themselves or others. This person will confide in those closest to them about the relationship looking for advice but unable to translate the advice into action. There is a sense of hopelessness that surrounds this person.

Think they can change the abuser. This is the person who honestly feels like they have the power and the ability to show their abuser that they can love them past their pain and be the person who pushes them into their greatness. They possess the "fix it" mentality and will put their abusers' feelings and needs in front of their own. They see the potential in their partner and will make them into their project to get them better. This person is determined to prove that they can create the relationship they have desired in their mind.

Lost their identity. This is the person who does not know who they are outside of their partner. They have forsaken the things that makes them unique to become the person that their abuser wants. They wear what the abuser likes, they are alienated from their family and friends, they don't have a mind of their own, and they have lost the power of their voice. For the sake of peace, this person is determined to make their partner happy by accommodating all their requests. Their self-esteem and self-worth is depleted; they are unable to think logically or clearly for themselves.

No exit plan. This is the person who wants to leave the relationship but does not know how to exit safely. The idea of starting over is completely overwhelming, and the fear of the unknown keeps them stuck in a toxic relationship. They fear their partner, so just walking out the door isn't an option. This person has a hard time making decisions because they have released all control to their partner. This person has not thought about what life will look like without their partner.

Love their partner. This is a person who loves their partner and is willing to stay with them, no matter what. They have decided to let their love be the glue that holds them together. This is the person who will blame themselves for their partners' behavior. They believe that they don't deserve anything better than what they have. They are determined to prove to their partner that they are loyal and will not abandon them. Since their identity is found within their abuser, they are unable to live without them. This person is determined to prove that they are enough for their partner.

Supporting Someone Involved in Domestic Abuse

Being an outsider looking into a relationship that is engulfed in domestic violence, your perspective is going to be logical, confident, and protective because you love the person being abused and you want what is best for them. Supporting someone in this type of relationship can be a bit hard at times. From your perspective, you will not understand why they are staying, why they are accepting this behavior, and why they just will not leave.

It will lead you to want to insert yourself in the situation and say, "I would not put up with this if I was you" or "This is ridiculous! This isn't the first time your partner has done this" or "If something else happens to you, I'm going to talk to your partner."

These statements will actually push your friend or family member closer to their partner instead away because they feel like they need to protect their relationship. I have found ways of support that are beneficial to helping someone involved in domestic abuse.

Love them. This is the time when you focus on building up their self-esteem and self-worth. By reminding them of who they are and what you love about them will help them find their identity again. Providing encouragement to your family member or friend will let them know that you love them despite their current situation.

They are expecting you to judge them or give your opinion on their relationship. By doing the opposite of what they expect will remind them of the difference between healthy and unhealthy love. Having compassion for someone can provide healing to inward wounds. You letting them know that you see them and they matter to you.

First John 4:18 says, "There is no fear in love. But perfect love drives out fear, because fear has to do with punishment. The one who fears is not made perfect in love." By taking the time to love your family member or friend, you are allowing them to experience the love of Jesus Christ, which will do more than you think. Trust me!

Don't try to fix their situation. When you find out that your family member or friend is involved in a domestic abusive relationship, the first instinct is to protect them by removing them immediately from the situation. Your mind is moving quickly, trying to find solutions to remedy their pain. Your temper begins to flare, and anger begins to take over. Calm down!

It's evident that you love them, but you cannot remove them from a situation that they are not ready to end. During this time, you have to allow them to make decisions for themselves and come up with a solution for ending their relationship. Your friend or family member may ask you for advice on what to do. It is important not to give them a list of things you would do and how you would do it.

The best thing to do is to counter their question with a question. A few examples would be "What do you think you should do?" or "What would you tell your daughter or someone you loved in this situation?" or "When you think about what you want from a relationship, are you receiving that?" Please give them time to think about their answers and not coach them to say what you want them to say.

You can provide helpful information for domestic abuse support groups, shelters, counselors, pastors trained in domestic violence prevention, helpful websites, etc. Don't set up the appointments; just let them know that you have additional information they can use when they are ready for extra help. Let them make the calls and set up appointments. When you allow them to do it, those actions give them strength and hope.

Speak life over them. Proverbs 18:21 states, "Death and life are in the power of the tongue, and those who love it will eat its fruit." God has given you the ability to reverse the negative comments that have been spoken over them in their abusive relationship, give courage, and provide inspiration to look past their current situation and no longer believe the lies they are being told by their abuser.

Your encouragement will be the give them the inner strength needed to make the call, go to the website, or move out. Your words are like a seed being planted in the grounds of their hearts. The more you supply them with positive affirmations, it begins to water the hope in their hearts; and next thing you know, courage is formed and a new mind-set is created. The way you encourage a baby who starts walking is the same way you want to encourage a person trying to leave an abusive relationship. They need compassion, patience, encouragement, hope, and strength.

Listen to them. For some people, this may be a tough request because you may get tired of hearing the same old story with no solution. James 1:19 says, "So then, by beloved brethren, let every man be swift to hear, slow to speak, slow to wrath."

Being in an abusive relationship will cause your family member or friend to lose their voice and not be heard by their partner. You provide them an avenue to inform them that their voice matters and they are important. Most of the time, they do not want your advice, but they need to process through the pain and hopelessness they are feeling. You do have the right to set healthy boundaries as to what you will listen to and how long you will listen to them.

It is good to repeat back to them what you heard so they can hear what is happening in their relationship. Sometimes, they do not realize the magnitude of what they are enduring until they hear what you repeat back to them concerning their relationship. By providing a safe space for them to speak, you are reestablishing trust between the two of you. Their abusive relationship can cause them to feel crazy by having someone who loves them, and their trust can let them know that they are not crazy and the things they are enduring are not right.

Pray for them. Prayer is a powerful tool that can help in any situation. James 5:16 says, "Confess your faults to one another, and pray for one another, that you may be healed. The effective, fervent prayers of the righteous man avails much." When you pray for your family member or friend being abused, you are going to God on her behalf, asking for guidance, comfort, solution, and protection on their behalf. You are asking for supernatural intervention into a situation that you have no control over.

You can pray with them or by yourself, either way you are letting them know that you are standing with them. Praying after you have just listened to their confession is beneficial to you because you are releasing the heaviness and weight of the situation to Jesus and you do not have to take it with you. Prayer provides strength, hope, love, and understanding. It is important that you do not preach to them during the prayer.

An example would be this prayer:

> Lord, please open Suzie's eyes to see that she is in a bad situation and she needs to leave that horrible, devil-filled man. Lord, give her the confidence to contact the support group because she needs it. We are praying for an exit strategy because she keeps saying, but she is not doing anything, in Jesus's name. Amen.

That prayer was ineffective because you were subtly telling her what to do in "Jesus's name." Every time your family member or friend crosses your mind, pray for them. You are changing lives by being obedient to prayer.

Tools for Overcoming Domestic Abuse

When it comes to overcoming domestic abuse, there are a plethora of ways to heal. Over the years, I used these tools to shift from being a victim to victorious over domestic abuse:

Admit that you need help. This is the first step of the healing process because it helps break down the walls that guilt and shame have erected in your life. This is when you have exhausted all your options and you realize that this situation is bigger than you can handle emotionally, spiritually, physically, or psychologically.

It is time to tell the truth! Not only are you telling the truth to others, most importantly, you are telling the truth to yourself. You will get the necessary support and help to get out of your current situation. By admitting that you need help allows you to gain the power back in your life. During this time, you remember who you are and what you deserve.

Your eyes are now open to the truth, and you see that this relationship is killing you and it will never be what you imagined in your mind. This is when you are willing to break up; move out; and utilize the phone numbers, websites, and shelter locations that you have been given by your family and friends. This is a huge step because you are launching into the unknown but you are worth it.

Psalms 107:19 says, "Then they cry unto the LORD in their trouble, and he saves them out of their distresses." You are not alone during this time. The moment you cry unto the Lord, He will bring people to help you get through this time. You have been alone for the majority of your relationship, but that is going to change when you ask for help. I am reminded of the time when I cried to God for help. He immediately started putting together a plan for me to become free.

Forgive yourself. When you decide to forgive, you are making a conscious choice to change your attitude about wanting revenge or resentment. Matthew 6:14–15 says,

> For if you forgive others their trespasses [their reckless and willful sins], your heavenly Father will also forgive you. But if you do not forgive others [nurturing your hurt and anger with the result that it interferes with your relationship with God], then your Father will not forgive your trespasses. (AMP)

You benefit from forgiving yourself because it stops you from continuously condemning yourself for the getting into a bad relationship.

If you choose not to forgive, you will always have the magnifying glass out looking at every little nook and cranny, overanalyzing every little detail since you don't trust your decision-making skills. Hoping that you get it right that time because you can't afford to fail again. Ask God what His intentions are and what things He wants you to have. Honestly tell God in words how you released your intentions to Him. Honestly tell Him the hurt in your heart and how you were crushed from the promise of it all, which didn't happen.

How do you forgive yourself when you are hurting so bad? Take time and process your emotions and the situation with God and trusted people (i.e., counselor, pastor, support group, family members, etc.). When I say *process*, I mean to cry out, talk through, get mad, and go through the forgiveness cycle. This process is not going to happen in twenty-four hours. Take the time that you need to heal. Forgiveness is not about letting the other person off the hook; it is about freeing yourself from allowing them to have power and control over you. You can forgive a person, and but don't have to include them back into your life.

Love yourself. In order to effectively love yourself, it is imperative that you embrace God's love for you. Since God is love, He is the only one who can give you the proper definition and understanding of His intention for love.

Jeremiah 31:3 says, "The Lord appeared from of old to me saying, Yes, I have loved you with an everlasting love; therefore with loving-kindness have I drawn you and continued My faithfulness to you." When you embrace God's love, you are opening yourself to experience an unconditional love that will never leave or forsake you. God's love can forgive those things that you think are unforgiveable. It's strong enough to hold you up when you are at your breaking point. He has a love that will fill every empty space in your heart and introduce you to the person that you were created to be.

The next part of loving yourself is identifying how you see yourself. There is an exercise that I have found to be very helpful for this process. I call it Lies, Fear, and Shame. Take some time and look at yourself in the mirror and make a list of the positive and negative characteristics that you see.

If the list is full of negative things, you need to ask yourself, "Who told me I was these negative things?" The next thing you need to discover are the lies, the fears, and the shame that is attached to the negative perception that you wrote down.

The *lie* would be the negative image. The *fear* is what *will happen* because of the lie. The *shame* is the *past situation* that has left you *believing the lie* and *afraid of the fear*. Finally, you have to discover the *truth* about your *identity through scriptures* that contrasts those negative statements and *rehearse* your new truth on a *daily*, maybe even *hourly*, basis until you begin to *believe it in your heart and mind*.

Change your mind-set. We tend to rely on past personal experience to understand love rather than what God says. If you had a bad experience with love, you may think that you are unlovable or incapable of loving people. That is not true! Your identity is not what you have experienced; rather, your identity is found in who Christ said you were.

Romans 12:2 states, "Don't copy the behavior and customs of this world, but let God transform you into a new person by changing the way you think. Then you will learn to know God's will for you, which is good and pleasing and perfect" (NLT). It is impossible to consistently behave in a way that is inconsistent with your character.

When changing your mind-set, it is important to bring those negative thoughts under subjection. Second Corinthians 10:4–5 states,

> For the weapons of our warfare are not carnal but mighty in God for pulling down strongholds, casting down arguments and every high thing that exalts itself against the knowledge of God, bringing every thought into captivity to the obedience of Christ.

You have the power and authority to stop yourself from thinking negative thoughts and change them into positive thoughts. Philippians 4:8 states, "And now, dear brothers and sisters, one final thing. Fix your thoughts on what is true, and honorable, and right, and pure, and lovely, and admirable. Think about things that are excellent and worthy of praise" (NLT).

Join a support group. This is so important! You cannot do this alone. By attending a support group, it helps remove the guilt and shame that surrounds this issue. It also affirms that you are not crazy because other women are sharing similar experiences. As a facilitator of a domestic violence recovery group, I have watched women transform right before my eyes and find the strength, self-esteem, friendship, and Jesus. In addition, it brings clarity to the issue of domestic violence. If you attend a Christian support group, they also provide biblical understanding and tools that will help you be woman God created you to be.

Build your relationship with Christ. Devote yourself to God to the same degree you would a relationship with a natural person. God is love, and in order to know real love, it is imperative to spend time with Him. Building spiritual disciplines can be done in a creative way, such as the following:

- spending time conversing with Him (prayer),
- rereading his love note to you (reading your Bible),
- finding your song and singing to him (listening to Christian music),
- being exclusively with Him (you are willing to be focused on only Him and not entertaining other men [especially the devil]), and
- presenting yourself nicely (self-care).

Dream again. Just because you have gone through something like this does not mean your life is over. Take some time to remember what you have always wanted to do and go after it. It is not too late to go back to school, get that degree, start that business, write that book, go on vacation, or start a new hobby. The sky is the limit; you are capable of doing anything that you put your mind too. Do not let anything or anyone stop you. Overcoming domestic violence is the first step to the rest of your life. Do not be afraid to dream again. You can make it! You can begin again!

Chapter 8

Transparency

After going through a major process of self-discovery, I began living a new life. It seemed like the world had opened up to me, and I was given another chance to live on purpose. After taking the time to do my work and discover who I am, I felt like I was ready to get back on the dating scene. I was determined to enter into a healthy relationship.

I met a guy who attended my church, and I was so into him. I made my declarations that I was celibate, and I told him what my standard was and I was ready. Well, mentally, I was ready; but physically, I was not. After spending a lot of time with this gentleman, I noticed we had a lot of chemistry. He was very accepting of my standard, but when he did not respond like I thought he should, I quickly found myself becoming more affectionate. I realized that it is easy to be celibate when no one is around but very hard when you have temptation knocking at your door.

Inwardly, I tried to keep my flesh under control, but a part of me wanted this affection without the boundaries that I set. I found myself getting sucked back into the unhealthy relationship cycle that I had been freed from. I noticed the more I gave into my flesh, the more the relationship started becoming unhealthy; and I slowly found myself emotionally back to the girl who was desperate for his love.

At the beginning of our dating relationship, the guy was emotionally open but slowly started backing off, becoming emotionally unavailable. We never officially became a couple, but in my mind, we were together. The idea of him being "the one" started swirling around in my head.

The more he pulled away, the more I craved his attention. There were times I would text him and he would be delayed in responding, but I looked on social media and he was active. I ignored all the red flags; that I was operating from an unhealthy place, and the red flags he was giving me showed that he just wasn't that into me anymore. I wanted the relationship to work, and I was determined to make it happen.

For me, I was in the mind-set of the broken woman who needed to prove her worth and love to a man. There are times when I wanted to blame the guy I was dating for being a dirty, lowdown dog and putting me in that situation; but I had to be honest with myself. He didn't force me to do anything, I made those choices to give into my flesh. I was not strong enough in my new identity to be 100 percent me. I assumed he wanted someone other than who I was, so I gave him that, which ultimately backfired. I remained in this unhealthy cycle for six months.

While spending time with this guy, I heard the Spirit of the Lord speak to me and say, *"This man is not going to marry you. Why should he? You have given him every part of you that he has yet to work for. You are worth more than this."*

I immediately sat up and told him that he needed to leave.

He asked, "What was wrong?"

I replied, "You just have to go," holding back tears. And as he left, I asked him, "Do you love me?"

A startled look came across his face. He started stuttering and then said, "I wouldn't be here if I didn't."

Knowing that he wasn't sincere, I needed him to combat what I heard in my heart, so I said, "Tell me."

He replied, "Tell you what?"

I said, "That you love me."

He waited for five seconds and then mumbled, "I love you," and quickly ran out the door. I knew he didn't love me, and I knew that it was over. I embarrassed myself for the last time, and I knew that it was time for me to love myself more than this man.

The next day, I felt like a failure. It took me years to get to the place that I am comfortable with myself, embracing a new mind-set, setting a standard; and then it took only six months to throw it all away.

Prayer for Help

I know that this season has been one of the hardest seasons of your life. When you are trying to do right, but wrong is always there. You just don't see a breakthrough coming any time soon. It's like everything is falling and the walls are coming down, but it's not in a victory. You feel defeated and the tears keeps falling; you're disappointed in yourself, disappointed at life—you're just disappointed.

By that point, I was looking around, asking, "Lord, what do I do? Everything I seem to touch keeps messing up. I don't know how to succeed or win. It feels like every other day is a good day. I am tired of struggling in everything! People are telling me they are praying for me, but it doesn't seem like it is working. I try to pray for myself, but I feel defeated. I am holding on to the promises spoken over my life to 'stay on the potter's wheel' or 'to bury it out of your sight.'

"I am nervous because my past is reappearing in front of me, and I cannot resist the temptation this time. In addition, I don't have enough money to cover all my expenses, and my finances are out of order. I am finding myself smiling to keep from crying, and my emotions are all over the place. I don't know what else to do."

Fred Hammond's "A Song of Strength" started playing in the chorus, "My life is broken and I don't know what to do. While I'm in this change help me remain, I will count on you." Tears began to stream from my eyes because there was someone in this moment who understands my struggle.

The song continues, "Hold on and wait just a little while, He'll bring a song of strength in the midnight, touch your lives with your loving hand." I started having a conversation with the music, and I said, "I've been waiting, and nothing is happening. When I am waiting, I am falling." The song continues, "Hold on, don't you ever let go, let my Jesus lead, I guarantee you he knows, when the road gets rough, the going gets tough, the hills are hard to climb, looking for peace of mind, hold on don't you ever let go."

"When I am ready to give up, what do I do?" I asked. "Am I to 'hold on and don't ever let go'? But I keep falling." The song replies, "Hold on and don't let go."

I said, "Lord, I feel like a disappointment. I need you to hold on and don't let go. Lord, I am not able to pay all my creditors."

"Hold on and don't you let go," the Lord responded.

"But, Lord, I feel like I am out of your will," I said.

His response, "Hold on, hold on, don't you ever let go. You still have God. You still know He is there. You still call on His name. You must hold on with all that you have. Yes, the night seems dark, but you hold on to God's unchanging hand. I don't care if you can't feel Him or see Him. It is imperative that you hold on to him."

Cry out to him and say, "God, help me, help me in my unbelief, help me when I am falling. God, your word says, 'Now unto him who is able to keep me from falling.' I need your strength to keep me from falling because I can't depend on myself. I need your strength, God, I need your courage, I need my mind to be your mind, your will to be my will.

"Take my heart and mold it into yours. Take my will and conform it to yours. Let my mind be transformed into yours because I can't do this by myself. I keep leaning to my own understanding. I keep getting off the wheel that you have instructed me to stay on. I need to be inside your will where there is safety. I want to abide under the shadow of your wing. I need your shelter, Lord. I don't know what else to do or say.

"I am being attacked in my dreams. It feels like the enemy is waging war on me, and I can't stand. I want to stand and do what is right. I want to do your will, oh God. I know you told me to bury it because the situation has become unburied and is in front of me. I have to rebury this situation, not just talk about burying it but actually go through the process of discarding it—this time, out of my sight. This time, when I bury it, I have to forget about it and be free from it.

"I need your freedom over this area of my life. I know that in you there is freedom. I am tired and weary, God. I have become a slave to my sins, and I want to be free. I don't like living in this place. I know that I am worth more than this. You have so much in front of me that is so great, yet I am living like a pauper instead of a princess. I want more than this, God.

"Help me to remain and go through this—not just get me out—but go through so I can see the salvation, Lord, and I know that I can wait on you. I will know that you are faithful to me. I'm asking you to change my perception of how I think you see me. Change my heart so that I won't be turned over to a reprobate mind or to the lusts of my flesh. I don't want to be in a situation that causes me to look at you differently. Or you decide that you can't use me because I am not ready or willing to move forward.

"You have told me that there are so many great things in store for me. So I am calling you, saying, 'Please don't pass me by.' As the Bible says in Mark 10, that blind Bartimaeus cried out to Jesus, saying, 'Son of David, have mercy on me.'

"He was in the middle of the crowd asking for mercy to be endowed on him. He didn't think that Jesus would hear him because he was deemed as unclean and on the roadside begging. He didn't know that you would even care since he did not look like everybody else and his story wasn't familiar. He didn't stand strong on every issue. But, Lord, I am standing here like blind Bartimaeus with just a little courage to say, 'I have nothing left to lose. I am at my lowest place, and I said, "Jesus, Son of David, have mercy on me. Have mercy on me."'

"I know I am doing wrong, God, but I need your mercy. I know I can't make it right, God, but have mercy on me, Lord. I am not ashamed to stand in the middle of the crowd and declare, 'Have mercy!' I will stand before you and say, 'Have mercy,' and fall on to my knees and say, 'Have mercy.' I will pray in the morning and say, 'Have mercy.' I will cry in my car and say, 'Have mercy, Lord Jesus. Have mercy on me.'

"Look past my faults, God, and see my needs. I need you right now, I need you. Please don't pass me by. This is not just out of guilt but of remorse. It is a genuine change of heart that I desire. Please replace my heart of stone for a heart of flesh. I need a full exchange—

your competence for my incompetence, your faith for my unbelief, your love for my emptiness, peace for my restlessness and anxiety, your trust for my despair—in the name of Jesus.

"I need to know that you love me and you like me and that I am yours. You said that you will never leave me or forsake me, but I know there are times that you get frustrated with me, but I say, God, please don't pass me by. I want to make it through this, I want to be what you called me to be. I want to know that you are the I AM in my life.

"I surrender, I submit to you being I AM in my life. I want to fulfill the purpose and the plan that you have orchestrated for me. I don't want be delayed by spending extra time in the wilderness because I didn't trust your word. I want to be obedient to you. I want to love you more than I love my flesh. I want to love you more than I love myself. I want to love you, oh God, with the depths of my heart. I want to love you like none other, Lord Jesus. Let your will be done in my life.

"Take everything that is not like you—I just want you. Teach me your ways that I may know your statutes. Teach me how to love, teach me how to love you, teach me how to love myself, teach me how to love others. I am in a relationship, and I'm not sure where it is going. Teach me how to love him, if that is what you want for me. If this is not what you have for me, then take him. Help me to be obedient to your will and your way. Help us to put you first in our relationship. We don't want to build something based on sin. I'm asking that you give him vision and clarity concerning our relationship.

"I realized that this relationship or any other relationship will not work out if I do not deal with the sin that is in my heart. The lust that has taken over my flesh has not been tamed. I pray that my flesh is crucified right now in the name of Jesus. Help me not depend on my past—which include jobs, successes, failures—to be a factor for my future. I need to bury these things out of my sight and stand still and do the things that you asked me to do.

"Help me weep over what is dead in my life and place everything in its rightful place. I have to do my part, and I know that it is going to cost me something. What is it going to cost me to be in your will? How do I break free from this place of torment? How do I do what you have asked me to do and not be overcome with fear?"

Deny Yourself

God has called you for a purpose, and He knew that you weren't going to be perfect. He knew that you were going to struggle. He knew that you were going to fall. He knew it was going to happen, but He still called you. He said that "I will never turn my back on you. I WILL NEVER TURN MY BACK ON YOU!" He loves you and doesn't care what happens; your heart is His. He wants you, needs you, and loves you. You are His child, and He will not let you go.

The Lord says, "You are mine, and I have called you to fulfill a purpose. You just have to go through the fire and endure the process. It is a hard process, but you just keep seeking my face, keep seeking my face.

"I don't care how many tears you cry, how many times you fall down, you continue to seek my face. You keep seeking my face and trying your best. You do your best, and I will do the rest. Just do what I have asked you to do. I never asked you to be perfect or without flaw. I asked you to pick up your cross and follow me. That is all that I want you to do is crucify your flesh, pick up your cross, deny yourself, and follow me.

"When you pick up your cross, it is not going to be light or easy. At times, it will be hard, but in order to accomplish that, you must deny yourself. I know it is hard to deny yourself because self-fulfillment is easy, but you are more than capable of resisting the desire.

"I cannot make you deny yourself. I need you to choose to deny yourself. I can't force you to do that. This is a decision that you must make on your own. You will have to deny yourself and say no to the desires of your flesh. Everything else will come together and work out. You will not have to worry about how to accomplish goals, how to make your name known, how to be great, how to change the world, or how to fulfill your destiny I'll take care of that. All I need you to do is to deny yourself.

"Deny your will, ideas, and plans. When you forsake them, you are going through the burial process. The next thing you do is to pick up your cross and follow me. That is your assignment. You know that I am not going to leave you—I got you. No need to worry about getting married. I already promised you that.

"You are overwhelmed trying to figure out your purpose, destiny, and the plan for your life. And all I need you to do is deny yourself. You must deny your motives and plans, the mind-set of wanting to do things your way and not trusting anybody. You have to deny that negative mind-set and how you see yourself in that negative connotation. You must deny the lies of the enemy and your sinful nature. Deny it, pick up your cross, and follow me. I will order your steps according to my Word. For I know the thoughts that I think toward you," says the Lord, "thoughts of peace and not of evil, to give you a future and a hope."

Singleness

I had a dream that had to do with singleness and being a prepared for marriage. The dream opens up with me heading a flight of stairs and entering a great room. There were two additional hallways on both sides of the rooms.

The great room had cream walls with white trim. The atmosphere was very welcoming, and the people who were in the space were all mingling with each other. An announcement was made for all the married men to proceed to the hallway on the right and the married women to the left hallway to pray for their spouses.

Almost half of the people in the room moved to the assigned hallways. All the singles were left in the room. I noticed that the ratio between men and woman was off. There were way more women than men in the room.

I found myself standing in a line of women. When the woman at the front of the line said a word, a man would respond to her, and they would come together and pray for each other. The next woman was at the front of the line; and once she spoke a single random word, a man would come to her, and they would stand off to the side and start praying for one another.

This happened a few more times before my turn came up. As I watched the women in front of me, I realized that not every man could hear what she was saying, and only the man who was anticipating her word would respond to her. So when I came to the front of the line, my experience was a bit different than the women in front of me.

Before I could say anything, a light-skinned man of African descent walked up to me and said, with a British accent, "You have a doctorate. I need to pray for you." He immediately grabbed my hand, and while this was going on, I noticed a darker-skinned man of African descent with dreads making consistent eye contact with me; and he started walking toward me but he was far away.

As he approached me, a woman jumped in front of him, and he started talking to her. I turned my attention back on the light-skinned guy who had my hand. Before we could pray, a woman came and ripped my hand out of his; and she proceeded to hold his hand and she gave me her hand. She gave me the "He is my man, back off" look.

I looked at the man, and he was completely oblivious to what was going on because his eyes were closed and he was praying. I looked to my left side, and I noticed that this man had a total of six women around him. I stood in the circle they created, completely confused and uncomfortable.

I look around the circle again, and all the woman in the circle all have wedding dresses on. I was so confused, so I said to myself, "What is going on?"

I then heard the Holy Spirit say to me to pray for those men.

At that moment, I realized that that was not just a dream but an intercession. I started to pray for both men based on what I saw. For the dark-skinned man with dreads, I had to pray for him to become aware of the distractions that are assigned to keep me from the very thing that he was pursuing. I prayed that his desires for destiny would become stronger than his desire to settle for what was in front of him. I prayed for courage to resist what was easy and I prayed for strength to endure the journey of getting to what he wants. I prayed that his eyes were open to the truth and they could stay focused on the assignment God has for him and not on the temporary things in front of him. I prayed that his faith level was raised to believe that he could actually have the desires of his heart.

For the light-skinned man who came to be with a circle of women, I prayed for his heart to be healed of all the souls and emotional ties that he is oblivious to. I prayed that God would open his eyes to uncover all the women who are attached to him and the boldness to be able to stand alone in his singleness and be okay with Jesus alone. I prayed for clarity to be given to him that will answer the question as to why the relationship that he really wanted to work wouldn't come to fruition.

Before I could continue praying, I heard the Spirit ask, "You see these women around him?"

"Yes." I responded.

"These women are not those he has slept with. These are his female friends who secretly are in love with him. They are waiting for him to realize that he could be 'the one' for them. They are willing to wait on him because they don't think that no other man will respond to them in a relational manner.

"The woman who removed your hand has been there the longest, and she has decided that he is her husband and she will do whatever it takes to keep him all to herself. She has been hurt before, and the only person she trusts is him. The sad thing about all these women is that this man is not and will never look at them in a relational manner. The qualities he is looking for are not found in any of those women."

My heart broke for those women because they were willing to stand in a circle with other women, sharing a man instead of standing alone, anticipating God's best for them. I immediately started praying for those women. I prayed for the self-worth and self-esteem of those women to be increased and the brokenness that they have experienced to be healed.

I prayed for their eyes to be opened to their awesomeness and the courage to be completely devoted to Jesus Christ. I prayed for God to wrap his arms around them so that they can experience real love. I prayed for them to realize and believe that they are enough. I pray that they are urged to go on a journey of self-discovery to find themselves and be the woman whom God has called and created them to be.

I woke up from that dream with extreme clarity. For many years, I lived as those women, holding on to and building false relationships with my male friends. I found comfort in their friendship and confused their niceness for interest.

When I struggled with my self-esteem and self-worth, I knew that if a relationship didn't work, I could always fall back on my male friends to give me the male attention that I desired. There was one in particular that I was rather fond of, and we would talk pretty regularly. He would always come to me with all his problems, and I would always help him through them. I knew what he wanted, needed, and desired.

In my mind, I knew that I was everything that he requested. He just needed to see it for himself. I wasn't willing to say anything because I wanted him to change our relationship. I was okay with being friends until he was ready because having a piece of him was better than not having any of him. However, that relationship that I wanted never happened, and I was left crushed.

While on my journey of embracing God's love, He revealed to me the unhealthy emotional cycle that I would find myself in when potential relationships with my male friends never blossomed into something long lasting. This cycle reminded me of a hamster running on a wheel. The only progress I was making was getting on and off of the wheel. I would stay off that hamster wheel for months but encounter a tough situation and end up back on the wheel wore out and drained.

The Lord spoke to my heart and said, "*I just want to show you want it is, so when it happens again, you will be aware that you are doing.*"

The cycle consisted of creating a false relationship, seek attention, breaking down, self-attack, depression, self-coping, and forgiveness.

Unhealthy Emotional Cycle

Creating a false relationship. This is when I like a man and those what-ifs begin to start running through my mind. I talk about him with my girlfriends, and he becomes my crush. I don't want to be in a relationship with anyone else but him because in my mind, we are the perfect couple. I would never tell him my feelings because I was afraid that he would reject me. So, secretly, I would hope he would see me and decide to pursue me, confess his love, or at least his interest. He is built up high in my mind, and this continues for a while.

Seeking attention. When I begin reaching out to him, it is a one-sided interaction. When I call him, either he doesn't answer. Or if he does, he will say he needs to call me back and never does. His actions are a clear sign that he is not that into me, but I find myself in denial. The denial comes from me referencing the false relationship I have created. Then I would sit around, wondering why he never calls back, so I go on social media and begin to see if he's been online and who he is talking to. When you realize that he has been online and doesn't call you back or he is talking to another woman, I am crushed. Again, he has no clue that this is all going on because I have created a false relationship with him. This part of the cycle plays off my own insecurities.

Breakdown. Once he finally calls or texts me back and we are conversing, the topic of relationship comes up, and my heart starts beating fast because I think that today is the big day. He is going to confess to me that he wants to be with me. I would throw out all kinds of hints that I am so interested and I will be perfect for him—only to realize that he never acknowledges any of my hints. And then it happens… he informs me that he is dating someone and the woman that he is looking for is someone else. I am an amazing friend, but there is a particular woman that he is looking for, and it is not me.

As devastation begins to set in, I swallow hard and congratulate him on his new relationship and say, "Keep me posted on your dating process," feeling like my whole world is now crumbling and my heart is ripped out of your chest—another reminder that I am not good enough for another man. As soon as this happens, my whole disposition begins to change and I begin to yield myself to the lies of the enemy.

Self-attack. Now I am extremely sad headed for a crying session, and all my insecurities begin to surface and I nourish them with the lies of the devil. The thoughts of "Will someone ever love me? I am unlovable because every man I liked never liked me back. What am I doing wrong? Will anybody ever want me because I am a hot mess?"

I tried to change my thoughts but I can't. I started recounting every failed relationship, every bad word someone said about me being needy. It finally gets so bad that I can't take the torture, and I want it all to go away so I succumb to depression and cry yourself to sleep.

Depression. The next day I would wake up with a huge cloud of depression is hanging over my head. There were times when I would barely want to look at myself in the mirror. The only thing I would see is an ugly woman who couldn't get a man to save her life. I struggled to get out of bed, and all I want to do is sleep my life away. During this time, the only thing I could hear were the constant stream of insults replaying in my mind. I was sad and needed the torment to stop so I reached out to some friends and they tried to help me though the process, but the enemy said they don't understand you. So I finish the conversation and get back to my thoughts of despair. I block myself off from the world and just watch TV or chat online to numb the pain.

Self-coping. This is when I realize that I need to satisfy the pain, so I decide to indulge in my coping mechanism. My mind-set at this moment is, since no one thinks I am worthy to be loved, that means I must satisfy myself to prove that I don't need anybody but myself. The act varies on the situation or how I feel in that moment. At times, it would be going shopping and doing some retail therapy or calling an ex to meeting up for a quickie. Another could be eating a plethora of desserts (tub of ice cream, cookies, cake, etc.), and after the fulfillment is over, I would come back to reality and even worse off than I started.

Forgiveness. After the torture is unbearable, the only thing left to do is to ask God for forgiveness because I have sinned against God. The enemy has just played me like the lotto and is laughing because I actually believed all his lies and sinned. I asked God to wash me and cover me with his blood, and I got back into fellowship with God by listening to gospel music or praying. I only asked God for forgiveness and never repented. There is a difference between the two.

Forgiveness is saying sorry for actions that were hurtful to another party. Repentance is identifying a wrong pattern and completely turning away from the actions. No wonder I was stuck in this cycle because I wasn't repenting.

If you are unable to identify with this cycle of destruction, ask God to reveal to you the cycle of destruction that you fall prey to every time. You want to do this so you are able to have God break the chains that are holding you as a hostage to this cycle and change your thought process so you don't enter this cycle again.

The first time I wrote out my cycle and saw exactly what happened, for the first time, I saw that my cycle had nothing to do with the guy but me not trusting God and His plan. Instead, I'm trusting myself and trying to fill my own needs. God showed me I created my own bondage. Sometimes, I am the one who picks up the chains and buckles them to my waist. I am fighting with depression, guilt, shame, lust, doubt, unbelief, and depression from this one situation.

I prayed this prayer determined to break this cycle:

> Lord, I ask that you terminate any sinful plans that have been placed in my womb that will infest my whole life and lead me to death. I want to live for you. I am ready to move for-

ward and allow you to break the chains so that my mentality can change. The biggest change must be done, not just with my lips but through my actions. I know that this process is going to be hard to overcome, but I know that you are living inside me, and through you, I can do anything.

As I stated before, I thought that God's love was sympathetic, until I realized that God's love is genuine, long lasting, and unchanging. When you don't understand or appreciate God's love, you are opening yourself up to be deceived by the enemy, just like I was. I needed God to do a love reprogramming in my mind so I can get out of the cycle of deception/destruction.

This is no place to feel bad or accept condemnation. It's time to start training your thoughts so that you don't continue making the same mistakes. God has opened your eyes to this so you can be a part of the healing process. This is more than just reading a few scriptures and praying a quick prayer. It is about going back and surrendering over to Godly thoughts and ideologies that you have accepted about yourself that are not true. More than ever, God wants you to be a married woman in love and helping a man build the kingdom of God. That's what He created you for.

Think about it. If God didn't have that planned out, why would the enemy be fighting you so hard on this issue? The enemy only fights to destroy what is going to stand in his way of taking control. Since John 8:44 identifies the devil as a liar, and when he lies, he speaks his native language since no truth is in him. We have grown accustomed to believing a lie and not believing the truth. The truth comes with freedom, and it is not forced on you. A lie comes with bad emotional feelings and is continuously forced on you. The only way to gain clarity in distinguishing a lie from the truth is to see how the outcome will correspond to your life.

When you are exposed to truth, its ultimate result is to bring life, peace, joy, love, and empowerment to you. It's important to understand your authority, potential, and self-worth when walking in truth. When walking in truth, you are assured and content with God being your source for everything.

Your goal is to be in relationship with God while being his image bearer. When you are exposed to a lie, you are unsettled, delusional, have low self-esteem, unsure, afraid of any and everything, you can't see positivity, and, most importantly, you are stuck in the past. The goal is to be miserable and mistrust God or anyone else.

You Matter!

You were created with purpose, and you matter in this world. You matter! God loves you, and He wants you to live a life poured out, not afraid of utilizing the gifts and the talents He has given. You are an overcomer, a disciple maker, proof that His ways are higher than ours and His ways will work.

Embracing His love will show others that He is real, He is loving, caring, compassionate, and slow to anger. You are the one whom He called to show forth in this world the great and mighty things that He can do. No, the heavens might not be opening up and the thunder might not be rolling, but every day, someone will see within your life that God is real.

When you realize you matter, you will begin to make different choices; you will see life so differently. You will learn to love yourself; you will not allow others to treat you in a way that is less than what He has called you to be. Your relationship with God will be enough for you.

He wants to be your everything. He gives you the will to live, the ability to love, and the desire to want to help change the world. Your story changes the world. Your ability to do great things changes the world. Your knowledge changes the world. If it is just going to work every day with a positive attitude, being on time and having integrity will affect the life of someone else around you. You matter!

I will continue saying it until you believe it. You're not always going to be the ugly duckling; you are not always going to be the one who is picked last. You will not always wonder if you are enough and used for your gifts and talents. You will start walking with your head up high, declaring, "God, I want and receive all that you have for me!" So when you read promises in scriptures, you will believe that they belong to you.

You are so much bigger than what you think and see in front of you. Your businesses are not taking off because you don't believe that you can do it. *You can do it!* You have greatness inside of you, and I want you to see it. When you embrace God's love, you will be able to do anything. I want to encourage you on your journey. Let this process be one of life-changing magnitude. It took me a long time to do this. I was so scared of the unknown, but I decided to release my old perspective and allow God to replace it with His truth and love.

Chapter 9

Victory in Action

I had a text conversation with my ex-boyfriend, and throughout the conversation, I was able to see the growth that I have experienced since we broke up. The conversation was light at first, but then he started going down memory lane concerning our relationship. He kept bringing up what were good memories for him but were hurtful memories for me.

Each time he tried to bring up the past, I had to remind him of the outcome of that situation. He would say, "I don't want to remember that part," and I found that to be interesting because the devil does the exact same thing. Each time he speaks to us about experiences from the past, he tries to draw us back to that place by reminding us of the good times and not the bad. Proverb 26:11 says, "As a dog returns to his own vomit so a fool repeats his folly."

When the temptation arises for us to go back to a place of bondage, we must remind ourselves of the true outcome and thank God for allowing us to see the tactics of the enemy and continue moving forward. While my ex was speaking, I found myself reflecting on the steps I have taken to further grow and develop my self-esteem, confidence, and morals so that I will not have to experience another hurtful situation.

It seemed like he kept trying harder and harder to get my mind stuck in the past by reminding me of the activities we both participated in and how they made us feel. At that moment, I noticed I was beyond that place in my life and those things did not interest me anymore. I was appalled that he would bring something like that up to me. I ended that conversation by resisting his advances, and sure enough, he stopped talking to me when he realized I was not moving.

This situation proved two scriptures to me. The first is James 4:7: "Therefore submit to God. Resist the devil and he will flee from you." The other is Ephesians 6:14: "Therefore take up the whole armor of God. That you may be able to withstand in the evil day, and having done all, to stand."

There was a time in life when I would have taken the bait of the enemy and found myself returning to the vomit of that past relationship. I am so proud of myself for focusing on developing my relationship with Christ, which has helped me to stand on truth instead of the past relationships. Once the conversation was over, I kept telling myself, "Sondra, you just passed another test."

I could have fallen, but I chose to believe God and focused on moving forward and not going backward. When I stood up for myself, I did not feel any rejection at all. I felt more victory than anything else. I now realized that I am in a place called victory. I know that the enemy is going to come back again to try to tempt me; but with God's grace, mercy, and authority, I will not fail but continue to stand my ground and remain in a place called victory.

Not even three hours later, I received yet another text from this same guy, and it was some kind of an apology for hurting me the way he did and a dig about me holding on to the past. I told him that we could be friends with boundaries. I don't talk to any of my male friends about sex, so I am not going to start with him.

When I get into those conversations, I still feel like I am separating myself from God, and I am not doing that anymore. I have grown up and at a different level in Christ. That type of behavior is not okay. I do not have time for that type of childish thinking.

To me, it was about him not getting his way and trying to make me feel bad for not going with his plans. This situation is a perfect example of healthy rejection. I have to decide if this person is going to help me move toward my goals or hinder me, and I can tell that this is something that will hinder me. So why go around a block that is not going to lead me anywhere? I cannot afford to make a mistake, and I must stay focused on the path that is in front of me. I have to continue to ask God to lead me so I do not depend upon myself to make the decisions of my life.

Prayer

Lord, I thank you for the growth that you have allowed me to experience. I can remember, a year ago, when I was begging him to stay with me and I would have compromised myself just to have some type of male attention. I was so lost and empty that I needed any type of validation to fill the empty parts of my heart. Now I am not looking for a man for the fulfillment because, God, you have filled the empty places in my heart and my focus is on you.

I am so grateful for going through the process of healing. Yes, it was very hard and scary, but I would rather go through that than be defined by a false sense of self. When I do enter into a relationship, I want it to be one that is healthy and complements me and I complement him. I want the relationship to be a place of growth and not a place of hindrance. I want God to be at the head of our lives and the head of the relationship.

For the first time, I want to remain pure throughout the relationship. I don't want any type of sex to be presented or manifested until I get married. In order for that to happen, I have made a commitment to God and bought a promise ring that I would remain celibate until I get married. So that means personal sex, phone sex, and intercourse are out of the question until I get married. I know that this has been a big area of downfall for me for a long time, and I am tired of falling.

Jude 1:24–25 says,

> Now to Him who is able to keep you from stumbling. And to present you faultless before the presence of His glory with exceeding joy, to God our Savior, who alone is wise, be glory and majesty, dominion and power, both now and forever.

This passage confirms that God can keep me from falling and the commitment made to God can be kept. I know that if I can stay committed to Christ, then I will be able to stay committed to my husband. I am learning the importance of my self-worth, and it is empowering. I trust God, and I know that all things are possible with Him. This interaction with my ex is really helping me to surrender more and more to God and trust that He will continue to lead, guide, and show me the way to go in this life.

I don't care if I sound deep, but I have to do whatever is necessary to maintain my sanity and my relationship with Christ. I love Him more than anyone else, and I don't care how anyone responds to my choices. I have to live my life for myself and for no one else, considering the ones who hurt me were looking out for themselves by leaving my situation even though I begged them to stay.

No more of that desperation. I know I am beautiful, and someone will find me, and we will be together. Until then, I will enjoy my Father and continue to let Jesus heal my heart from all the painful holes that have been placed in it. I will trust and love again, only when the time is right. The more I trust and love God, the more He will trust and love me. My life is not the same, and I will let it all go to live for God.

About the Author

LaSondra Barnes, M.Div., is the founder and CEO of Royal One Enterprise, LLC. As a life and spiritual coach, her mission is to provide a partnership that encourages and inspires women to discover and unlock their full potential. Her desire is to empower women to embrace God's love and understand their self-worth. Currently, she resides in Portland, Oregon, where she serves as a youth pastor at Life Change Church and an adjunct professor at Western Seminary.

LaSondra received her bachelor's degree from Michigan State University and a masters of divinity from Western Seminary. She is working on her doctorate in ministry at George Fox University.

CPSIA information can be obtained
at www.ICGtesting.com
Printed in the USA
BVHW030755240222
629774BV00025B/599